NEW
WORLDS
OF THE
UNEXPLAINED

by
Allen Spraggett

A SIGNET BOOK
NEW AMERICAN LIBRARY
TIMES MIRROR

COPYRIGHT © 1973, 1974, 1976 BY TORONTO SUN SYNDICATE

Ⓢ SIGNET TRADEMARK REG. U.S. PAT. OFF. AND FOREIGN COUNTRIES
    REGISTERED TRADEMARK—MARCA REGISTRADA
    HECHO EN CHICAGO, U.S.A.

SIGNET, SIGNET CLASSICS, MENTOR, PLUME AND MERIDIAN BOOKS
are published by The New American Library, Inc.,
1301 Avenue of the Americas, New York, New York 10019

FIRST PRINTING, FEBRUARY, 1976

1 2 3 4 5 6 7 8 9

PRINTED IN THE UNITED STATES OF AMERICA

For my son Stephen,
conservative Taurean
with a passion for crazy
hats. Long may he wear
them . . .

Introduction

When that pair of eccentric British geniuses, Alfred North Whitehead and Bertrand Russell, were collaborating on their masterpiece *Principia Mathematica,* Whitehead said to his younger protegé, "You know, Bertie, there are only two kinds of thinkers. The simpleminded and the muddleheaded.

"You, Bertie, are simpleminded. I am muddleheaded."

Well, Bertrand Russell went on simplifying until he became an agnostic materialist for whom the universe was a puzzle that made little sense. Alfred North Whitehead muddled on until he became a mystic for whom the universe was at once a profound and wonderful mystery.

I'm with Whitehead. As one of the muddleheaded I rejoice that there are things the simpleminded can't explain.

Hooray for the embarrassing data that no scientist knows what to do with, that don't fit in! Huzzah for the locks that have no known keys (nor ones we can even imagine)!

In this age of the computer and the robot, let's give a cheer for chaos, confusion, and marvelous disorder!

To have the universe neatly tucked into bed, with nothing sticking out—*that,* as Whitehead said, would be "incredibly boring."

I've spent years now exploring the sorts of things that drive the simpleminded mad. UFOs. Monsters. ESP. People who remember past lives. Trances. The mind mangling metal.

The weird, the strange, the unclassifiable—these are my delight.

The true stories in this book depict special people, places, and events which prove again that somewhere between science and superstition . . . the known and the unknown . . . the highest of man's hopes and the deepest of his fears is a profound and wonderful mystery.

Welcome to *New Worlds of the Unexplained!*

Contents

PART II. *Mysteries of UFO's*

PART III. *Mysteries of Faith and Healing*

PART IV. *Mysteries of ESP*

PART V.   *Mysteries of Ghosts and Messages From the Dead*

PART I

Mysteries of Nature

1. The Devil's Triangle

Within a roughly triangular area bounded by a line drawn from Florida to Bermuda to Puerto Rico and back to Florida, more than a thousand persons have disappeared in the past 20 years.

Most of these missing persons were aboard boats or planes which vanished.

The "devil's triangle," as it's romantically called, has a singular history of unsolved disappearances, though much of the area is only a hundred miles or so from the Florida coast.

On December 5, 1945, five Avenger torpedo bombers took off from the Fort Lauderdale Naval Air Station on a routine patrol flight. An hour and a half later the patrol leader radioed his base: "This is an emergency. We seem to be off course. We cannot see land, repeat, cannot see land ... Even the sky looks funny ..."

That was the last message. The whole patrol vanished and in spite of a massive search by 21 surface vessels and 300 planes, not a trace of the five planes was found—no debris, no bodies, not even an oil slick.

The disappearance was inexplicable because flying conditions were perfect and all the crews had made the same patrol innumerable times.

On August 28, 1963, two four-engine military jets left Homestead Air Force Base near Miami on a classified refueling mission over the Atlantic. Last radio contact showed the planes to be 800 miles northeast of Miami and 300 miles west of Bermuda. Then, on a clear day, the planes vanished.

Same story. No debris, bodies, or oil slick, despite an intensive sea and air search.

One of the most recent reported disappearances in the devil's triangle involved a light plane piloted by Carolyn Cascio, which left Pompano Beach, Florida on June 8, 1969 with a male passenger aboard.

The plane stopped at Georgetown in the Bahamas for refueling, then left for Grand Turk Island about 250 miles away. Three hours later the Grand Turk airport got a radio message from the plane that the direction-finding equipment wasn't working properly.

The pilot said she was circling "two islands and nothing is down there." Guests at a hotel in Grand Turk saw a plane circling overhead at that time. The light was still good, and the hotel should have been visible from the air.

The plane wheeled aimlessly in the sky for 30 minutes. Then the pilot radioed, "I'm out of fuel."

After that—nothing. Searchers found no trace of the plane or passengers.

This case is typical. Most disappearances in the devil's triangle involved good weather. In most instances the planes' navigational aids seemed to malfunction. And, as has been intimated, usually no trace is found.

There have been suggested explanations.

Could the devil's triangle be an area where from time to time freak atmospheric conditions develop—violent winds, say—which tear the craft to bits? Weather experts say no.

Another suggestion is that the area may be a "gravity sink"—a spot where, for unknown reasons, gravity occasionally goes haywire and sucks craft into a vortex of turbulence which destroys them.

It's even been speculated that the missing planes may have entered a space warp—a sort of hole in space leading to ... what?

The devil's triangle is part of the unexplained.

2. The Strange Deaths of Astral Twins

"There is a time to be born and a time to die," the Bible says. This is the story of two men, unrelated by blood, who shared a strangely similar destiny.

The story began back in 1968, when I received a letter, dated October 25, from John M. Brown of Gormley, Ontario. That letter is before me now as I write. Let me quote part of it:

"Although I am skeptical about astrology, this letter, strangely enough, has to do with that subject.

"In 1955, at the age of 41, I had the relatively unusual experience of meeting and working in the same office with a man who was born the same day and year I was born, i.e., July 22, 1914. Although we made no comprehensive effort to compare our experiences the following facts emerged.

"1. We were both employed in the accounts department of the Ontario department of public works.

"2. We both had taken secretarial courses, including shorthand, rare for men.

"3. We both had worked in army orderly rooms during the Second World War.

"4. We both had worked on Patrick Street in Toronto.

"5. We both had worked on Front Street in Toronto.

"6. We both had married women born in February.

"7. We both had married women from another province.

"8. We both owned American Motors automobiles.

"9. We both weighed 190 pounds.

"10. Both our surnames started with the letter B.

"I suppose the final evidence will be provided if both our names appear in the death columns the same day. It is unpleasant to dwell upon but gives one cause for conjecture . . ."

The curious sequel to this letter came on September 26, 1972, when I received a note from Mr. Brown's wife. She wrote:

"Another strange parallel between my husband and the other man developed recently. The other man died on September 22, 1972, two months after my husband's death on July 24.

"They didn't make it on the same day, but two months apart seems significant enough."

Mrs. Brown enclosed an obituary which said her husband's time-twin had died at age 58. "Suddenly."

She concluded her letter: "By the way, both men were buried from Trull Funeral Home in Toronto, and this was not by design on the part of the widows, since we have not been in touch since about 1958."

And so the strange parallels go on.

3. The Stars and Your Occupation

Does your birthdate have anything to do with the sort of job you have?

In 1950, a French social psychologist named Michel Gauquelin was doing research with the intention of debunking astrology once and for all. To Gauquelin, a graduate of the famed Sorbonne in Paris who now teaches at the University of Strasbourg, the notion that the heavenly bodies can influence human affairs was a silly superstition, unworthy of a scientific age.

He wanted to show conclusively that there was no correlation at all between a person's birthdate and hour and anything else concerning him.

However, the young psychologist came up with some embarrassing findings.

One of Gauquelin's research samples consisted of the birthdates of 576 members of the French Academy of Medicine. Curiously enough, he found that a significant number of them were born when Mars and Saturn were rising in the sky.

(The meaning of this phrase "rising in the sky" is simple enough: Because of the earth's daily rotation on its axis, the planets—like the sun and moon—appear to come up in the east, climb in the sky until they reach a highest point, then slowly descend and pass below the horizon in the west.)

Why should so many of these doctors have been born when Mars and Saturn were rising? The coincidence bothered Gauquelin. So he assembled a second sample of 508 eminent physicians.

After analysis, the same strange correlation showed up: An abnormally large number of these medical men, too, were born when Mars and Saturn were rising. Statistically, it seemed out of the question that this was merely a chance relationship.

To make absolutely certain, Gauquelin did a massive study using the birthdates of 25,000 Europeans—not only doctors this time but writers, actors, politicians, athletes, military

men, and other professionals. Incredibly, when these birthdates were put through a computer, statistically significant oc-
cupational groupings emerged.

Sure enough, the doctors were mainly born when Mars and
Saturn were rising. Professional soldiers were born mainly
when Jupiter was rising, scientists when Saturn was rising, politicians and writers when the moon was rising, and professional athletes when Mars was rising.

Psychologist Michel Gauquelin was astounded. The odds
against this correlation between a person's birthdate and his
occupation being due merely to chance were, in some cases,
five million to one!

That the link does exist appears statistically unassailable.
But explaining it—well, that's another matter . . .

4. The Murderous Moon

Shakespeare wrote about the inconstant moon, but what
about the murderous moon?

A psychiatrist and a psychology professor at the University
of Miami have come up with evidence that murders are
correlated with the phases and positions of the moon.

According to Dr. Arnold Lieber and Professor Carolyn
Sherin, the number of homicides significantly increases at the
times of the full and new moon, and such crimes tend to be
more vicious when the moon is nearest the earth.

Traditionally, of course, it was under the full moon that
vampires, werewolves, and similar charming creatures walked
abroad. And the term "lunatic" originally meant one who had
a "tic" (or twitch) of the moon.

Now scientific research is revealing that moon madness is
more than a popular superstition.

For their research Drs. Lieber and Sherin used about 2,000
homicides committed in the greater Miami area during the
15-year period up to and including 1970. The data came
from the files of the Dade County, Florida, medical exam-
iner. As a cross-check, 2,000 homicides for the 13-year period
1958-1970 were taken from the files of Cuyahoga County
coroner's office in Cleveland, Ohio.

The researchers wanted to test two related hypotheses: That the murder rate coincides with the phases of the moon: and that it coincides with the periods of the moon's maximum gravitational influence.

(The moon's gravitational effect increases with that body's nearness to the earth, reaching a peak when it's at its closest point, or perigee.)

The results of the study showed that the frequency of homicides correlated strikingly with the lunar phases. Murders escalated under the full and new moon.

There was no evident correlation between the moon's nearness to the earth and the murder rate. Interestingly enough, however, the study did show that homicides committed when the moon's gravitational force was at its maximum were "often of a particularly bizarre and ruthless nature."

In other words, while the moon's phase relates to how many murders are likely to be committed, its position relates to how vicious these will be.

Could these findings be some freak coincidence, mere chance? Not likely. The increase in homicides was noted in both Florida and Ohio. However, it was less dramatic in Ohio than in Florida, leading Dr. Lieber to conclude that "geographical location is a significant factor" in lunar influences.

How the moon affects you depends, it seems, on where you are.

How do the pair of scientific researchers explain their curious findings?

They suggest that since the moon regulates ocean tides and the human organism is 80 percent water it's only natural to expect "biological tides" within the body. These may alter body metabolism and brain chemistry in such a way as to trigger outbreaks of violence in susceptible persons. And violence may lead to murder.

And so the evidence continues to pile up that man, for good or ill, is linked to the cosmos by innumerable invisible threads. . . .

5. They Used to Call It Palmistry

Ever notice how ideas that science kicks out the front door have a way of returning by the back door?

A case in point is what used to be called palmistry. It's back now as the new science of "dermatoglyphics"—the study of palm and finger markings (or even the ridges on the soles of the feet), which, properly interpreted, can reveal many physical and psychological conditions.

Mental illness, retardation, certain birth defects, even a tendency to criminal behavior—all these and more are said to show up in an individual's dermatoglyphics.

Studies by Dr. Carol Baker, chief psychologist at the Des Moines, Iowa, Child Guidance Center, indicate that a child's fingerprints may reveal whether or not he'll turn out to be a criminal.

Although everyone has his or her own unique fingerprints, they come basically in five patterns—plain arch, tented arch, radial loop, ulnar loop, and whorl. The fingerprints of criminals convicted of rape, murder, or manslaughter had a higher number of ulnar loops and a lower number of whorls than those of noncriminals.

Curiously, criminals convicted of armed robbery showed distinctive differences of their own—more plain arches and fewer whorls.

A possible link between palm prints and schizophrenia, the serious mental illness popularly called "split personality" was uncovered by researchers at Michigan's state hospital in Ypsilanti.

Dr. Theodore Raphael compared the hand prints of 100 male schizophrenics with those of 5,000 normal men and found distinctive "whorls and arches" not shared by the normals.

The American Medical Association officially lauded the research as "accenting the significance and value of dermatoglyphics for medicine as a clinical tool and genetic lead."

The term "dermatoglyphics" for palm and finger markings was coined in 1926 at Tulane University, New Orleans, by

Dr. Harold Cummins. And it was at Tulane that doctors recently established a link between fingerprints and certain forms of congenital heart disease.

Drs. Alfred Hale, John Philips, and George Burch compared the fingerprints of 157 patients suffering from congenital heart disease with those of a similar number of patients with heart disease that developed in later life.

Certain peculiarities were noted in the first group not found in the second.

British psychiatrist Dr. L.R. Penrose, a pioneer in dermatoglyphics, says a telltale mark of mongolism (a severe form of mental retardation, also called Down's syndrome) is the so-called "simian crease"— a groove running straight across the palm. This occurs rarely among normal people but is common among mongoloids. (However, two men I know, both highly intelligent and one a millionaire, have such a simian crease!)

Dr. Fred Rosner, an epidemiologist in Washington, D.C., employed by the U.S. Public Health Service, is seeking links between dermatoglyphics and such neurological disorders as epilepsy and cerebral palsy. He said there may also be forewarnings of cancer in a person's palm print, either because the hand indicates a type of genetic makeup known to be predisposed to the disease or because the actual onset of the disease causes changes in the hand.

The leading scientific exponent of what is called "chiropsychology"—the psychology of the hand—is Dr. Charlotte Wolff, an English clinical psychologist whose doctorate is from the University of London.

She claims to be able to assess an individual's character and personality from his palm print.

In one test, Dr. Wolff described the temperaments, talents, and intelligence of a group of schoolchildren she had never seen solely on the basis of their palm prints in ink. Her comments were then compared for accuracy with assessments of the same children made by a psychiatrist after personal interviews and study of their records.

The results?

"The agreement is complete," said the psychiatrist in most cases. Or, "these are two pictures of the same child."

6. The Loch Ness Monster Returns

Monster pictures tend to be a dime a dozen, and most are palpable fakes. But somebody has taken an underwater photograph of the famous Loch Ness monster that has the experts frankly shaking their heads.

They consider the picture the best evidence yet for what a growing number of investigators have come to suspect—that there really is something huge, alive, and presently unclassifiable prowling the murky depths of Scotland's biggest lake.

Last year a Boston-based team of investigators who call themselves the Academy of Applied Science spent the summer camped on the shores of Loch Ness, determined to bring back, if not "Nessie" (as the monster is called), then at least tangible evidence of her existence.

They got the next best thing to the monster herself—a photograph of part of her anatomy.

Monster-watching at Loch Ness is a tedious business because, though there have been hundreds of sightings, Nessie is shy and her public appearances tend to be brief and furtive. Therefore, the 12-man investigating team decided to invade her watery domain with an eye that never sleeps.

Using a special strobe camera developed by Professor Harold Edgerton of The Massachusetts Institute of Technology, they set a photographic trap for the monster under a large school of salmon.

On August 8, between 1:40 and 2:10 A.M., something slithered through the trap. A sonar record (made by bouncing sound waves off the target) showed what appeared to be two undulating objects, each about 30 feet long, with many smaller objects, assumed to be fish, scurrying away. At the same time the strobe camera caught an amorphous shape that seemingly was rough-textured and greenish-brown in color.

One of the photographic images looked like the huge fin of some giant fish.

Scientists who've studied the photographs and the sonar record admit to being impressed.

"The sequence appears to show the passage of a large object, and the films are genuine underwater photographs," allowed J.G. Sheales of the British Museum of Natural History.

"The animal or animals in the photograph have a dimensional extent of approximately 20 to 30 feet," judged oceanographer Paul Skitzi.

"The creature has several segments or projections, such as humps," commented underwater sonar expert Martin Klein of Salem, New Hampshire.

The president of the monster-hunting Academy of Applied Science, Boston attorney Robert Rines, says he's convinced Nessie exists—and probably more than one, for breeding purposes. There have, after all, been reports of the monster for at least 1,500 years, and it's unlikely any creature could be that long-lived.

What could the monsters (assuming they exist) possibly be?

The most likely guess is some sort of aquatic creature from the paleozoic age whose great-great-grandparents got into Loch Ness millions of years ago before it was cut off from the ocean. The lake, 25 miles long and teeming with fish, is quite capable of providing sanctuary for a respectable family of monsters.

The notion of prehistoric sea serpents surviving into the twentieth century is made more plausible by the startling discovery a few years ago of a live coelocanth—a fish thought to have been extinct for 30 million years. (Since then, several specimens of this "living fossil" have been caught.)

However, there are people who don't think the Loch Ness monster is really a monster at all.

There have been suggestions, apparently serious, that it's an underwater UFO lurking in the lake for mysterious purposes of its own.

An even more exotic theory comes from British writer F.W. Holiday, who says the monster may be something more like a demon. In June, Mr. Holiday took a Church of England vicar, the Reverend Dr. D. Ormand, to Loch Ness to perform a rite of exorcism.

There are no reports of Nessie having been seen since.

7. The Ghostly TV Signal

Most of us know about "ghosts" on television—the fuzzy images that turn up when reception is lousy or a tube is getting ready to burn. But can a TV signal itself have a ghost?

For a while it seemed that the answer might be yes.

The mystery, one that remained unsolved until recently, started back in 1953 when somebody in England reported picking up on their television screen the call letters of TV Station KLEE in Houston, Texas.

Now this was before satellites, remember, so transatlantic television reception was something pretty startling. But what made the people in Houston really sit up and take notice was that the call letters of KLEE had not been broadcast for more than three years!

Station KLEE had been on the air from May, 1949, to the middle of 1950, then was sold and changed its call letters to KPRC (which is still going strong in Houston as Channel 2).

How, then, could somebody claim to have picked up the KLEE test signal three years after it had last been broadcast?

Could that television set in England possibly have tuned in on a signal from out of the past? If so, where had the signal been for three years—wandering around in space, bouncing off some distant star, intercepted and relayed back by a UFO maybe?

Engineers at Station KPRC in Houston received from England a number of photographs that clearly showed the call letters KLEE on a television screen. Accompanying one of them was a letter that said: "This photograph was taken by an ordinary box camera of what I believe is your test signal received at 3:50 P.M., September 14, 1953. Please confirm or deny that it is your signal."

The engineers at KPRC noted that the TV image in the photos—which showed the letters "KLEE" and underneath two diagonal lines—was very similar to the actual test pattern, but there were several details missing. Maybe these had somehow gotten lost in the freak transmission, or were so blurred they weren't visible.

One engineer at KPRC suggested the signal in the photos might actually be part of a Kleenex commercial that somehow flew across the Atlantic. A check, however, failed to find evidence that any such commercial had been used on that date and time by a major television outlet in the States.

The British Broadcasting Corporation heard about the case, looked into it, and said they were stumped. Engineers at the Chrysler Corporation investigated it and concluded the case was genuine—that somehow a TV image had been received three years after it was transmitted.

Reader's Digest wrote about the television signal that got lost in time. Then the story started turning up in books about UFO's and soon became a favorite of mystery-mongers.

After all, what could be more mysterious than a television signal from the past?

However, there are mysteries and pseudo-mysteries, and the latter tend to shrivel under careful scrutiny. This is what happened when Dr. Frank Drake looked into this case.

Drake, professor of astronomy at Cornell University, revealed his findings at a scientific symposium at that university. The truth, he said, is that the TV signal from the past was a hoax.

It was perpetrated, he suggests, by an Englishman who was trying to sell his countrymen "super-TV" sets, supposedly capable of picking up programs from the U.S.

To prove his claims, says Drake, the hoaxer faked the test signals of several American television stations—and one in Moscow too—and sent them photos with a request for confirmation that their call letters really had been picked up in England on his super-TV set.

Obviously, when the hoaxer faked the test pattern for Station KLEE, he didn't know it had changed its signal three years before. Instead of this exposing the hoax, however, as one might have expected, it was hailed as an even greater mystery.

With Dr. Drake's revelations, a phony mystery bites the dust.

But there are many real mysteries left to tantalize and amaze us.

8. Atlantis Revisited

There have been recent news stories reporting the discovery of myth-shrouded Atlantis in the Mediterranean and in the Atlantic off the coast of Spain.

But Manson Valentine thinks he's found part of the lost continent in the Bahamas.

Valentine, a distinguished-looking man with steel-gray hair and mustache, is a reputable scientist. He has a Ph.D. in zoology from Yale, has taught at several universities, was curator of the Alabama Museum of Natural History, and is now honorary curator of the Science Museum of Miami.

The underwater ruins he discovered in 1968, with noted oceanographer Dmitri Rebikoff, lie somewhere between the islands of Bimini and Andros. They could be, says Valentine, the first tangible remnants of fabled Atlantis.

He believes that the lost continent was historical not mythical and comprised several large land masses in what is now the Atlantic Ocean. These were submerged 10,000 to 15,000 years ago, he suggests, in a chain-reaction of stupendous natural convulsions.

In 1969, when Valentine first told me about the underwater site, it consisted of only six buildings in a small area. Now it has been found to be "a vast metropolitan complex covering thousands of acres."

The central building of the original group, tentatively identified as a temple, has stone walls three feet thick and a style of architecture known as cyclopean. Its dimensions are 100 feet long and 60 feet wide, roughly those of a surburban house lot.

Valentine has photographs of stone monoliths, as big as automobiles and evidently man-made, which extend in parallel rows for miles under the ocean. Aerial photos he showed me depicted enormous circular shapes, thought to be structures, clearly visible in deeper water.

More recently, fluted columns and what appears to be the tip of a giant step pyramid protruding from the ocean silt have been discovered at a depth of 20 feet.

How old are the ruins?

"We consulted Professor Nesteroff of the Sorbonne, one of the world's leading marine archeologists," said Valentine, "and by carbon-dating he estimated fossil mangrove material associated with the ruins at the 12-foot level to be 6,000 years old.

"Those at 20 feet are much older, indicating that the structures at that depth may go back 12,000 years.

"That would make it the oldest archeological site in the world."

The discoverers of underwater ruins are often reluctant to reveal the exact location of their find, to be sure that they retain control of the investigation. However, outsiders inspected some of the sites described by Valentine and Rebikoff.

These outside investigators suggested that some of the "ruins" are merely natural formations, while others are turtle or sponge pens built recently by the local Bahamians or, at the earliest, by the Lucayan Indians who inhabited the area when Columbus arrived.

Certain so-called ancient stone columns from the sea bottom proved on closer investigation to be merely cylindrical cement ballast.

However, Valentine insists that the site has authentic ruins. He points out that the Lucayan Indians could hardly have built the underwater structures since, so far as is known, they did not work with stone.

"Moreover," he said, "while some of the structures may indeed have been used as turtle crawls of the local people, the structures themselves undoubtedly are symbolic in design. Some, for instance, are hexagonal, and one is shaped like an immense sword."

Atlantis, in Manson Valentine's view, was a glamorous civilization advanced technologically beyond any known ancient culture. It sank from history after a series of unimaginably violent cataclysms, including volcanic eruptions, submarine earthquakes, and titanic tidal waves.

During its death throes, refugees streamed to various parts of the world—Egypt, sections of Europe, and Central and South America. In these latter areas they seeded the advanced cultures of the Incas and Mayas.

These Atlanteans, Valentine speculates, were predominantly light-skinned, and in the Americas intermarried with the dark-skinned Indians who probably came later.

"There are intriguing bits of evidence to support this," he

said. "Pizarro found blond and red-headed Incas, and the lighter their color the higher up the social scale they were. The gods of ancient Mexico, too, were bearded and white."

There were linguistic clues suggesting a common Atlantean origin for widely separated cultures, Valentine claims.

"Artifacts have been found on an island in the mouth of the Amazon bearing inscriptions in a language which is Cretan or Greek in nature. In Northern Brazil there is a tribe today whose language shows remnants of Etruscan, the tongue of pre-Roman Italy."

And so beneath the clear azure waters near Florida lies an unresolved mystery.

Freakish natural formations which look like buildings? Remnants of an early American culture similar to that of the Mayas and Incas?

Or, just possibly, tangible evidence that a myth has become reality?

9. Do Plants Have Emotions?

Cleve Backster believes that plants can perceive love and pain and become emotionally involved with people.

You may have heard of Backster. He's the man who first hooked up a plant to a lie detector.

Yes, that's what I said—a lie detector. And he claims the plant reacted with "humanlike responses" indicating "primary perception."

In other words, the plant showed emotions.

Oh, I know it's crazy. But so is a man walking on the moon. So let's listen to what Backster has to say before making up our minds.

Backster, a New Yorker, is a genial, middle-aged authority on the use of the polygraph (or lie detector.) In fact, he's tops in his field, having served as polygraph consultant to the Central Intelligence Agency and numerous law-enforcement organizations, including the FBI.

Not long ago I heard him talk about his off-the-beaten-track research.

Backster explained that, in normal use, the polygraph

works by detecting the subject's emotional reactions to questions as indicated by changes in his bodily functioning.

One device measures breathing rate and blood pressure. Another (the one Backster uses on plants) measures the "galvanic skin response." This refers to "changes in the person's electrical potential which cause the polygraph recording to go up and down in relation to his emotional state."

Put simply, the subject attached to a polygraph causes a pen to trace wiggly lines on a graph, and as long as he's emotionally unruffled these lines are fairly even. But if he shows strong emotion, as when asked about a crime he's involved in, the pen makes a sudden leap.

Polygraphists call such a leap "a threat-to-well-being response."

Well, Backster said that when he attached the electrodes of a polygraph to the leaf of a plant in his office, a common philodendron, and then threatened to burn the leaf—the pen took a leap. He interpreted this as a sign that the plant was reacting to his threat with fear.

Wait a minute, you say. What was Backster doing hooking up a plant to a polygraph in the first place? What gave him the idea?

Good question. Knowing that the whole business would sound pretty strange to some people, Backster at first invented a "cover story."

He was trying to measure the rate of moisture absorption by the plant, he said. Now he admits the truth: "I don't have the faintest idea why I did it."

Further research yielded even stranger results.

Backster says he found that his philodendron reacted emotionally to the death of other living things in its environment. So he set up an experiment using brine shrimp as the sacrificial victims.

"One reason for picking them was that there's no Society for the Prevention of Cruelty to Brine Shrimp," Backster said with a wry smile.

"Thus far I've received only one why-are-you-killing-those-poor-brine-shrimp letter."

The shrimp were put to death by being dumped into boiling water. Time and time again, it was found, at the moment the shrimp hit the water the nearby philodendron "showed a violent polygraph reaction."

Backster says he also discovered evidence of telepathy between him and his philodendron.

"We have found," he said, "that whenever I am away on a speaking engagement, even if it's a thousand miles from New York, the moment I flash on the screen a slide of the philodendron that started it all, there is a very dramatic reaction by the plant back in the lab.

"We've done this many times. I've coordinated it very carefully with my associate who attaches the electrodes to the philodendron. I keep a stopwatch record of the time that the picture of the plant is flashed on the screen.

"At that very instant, back in New York, the polygraph pen takes a leap."

The plant, in other words, knows it's being talked about. Or so Backster interprets the phenomenon.

What do other researchers say about such claims?

One who says he's substantially duplicated Backster's results is Dr. Aristide Esser, a psychiatrist at the research center of Rockland State Hospital, Orangeburg, New York.

"When I first heard of Backster's experiments I laughed it off," he said, "but I've had to eat my words."

Other researchers, however, say they have gotten very different results. Dr. George Owen of Toronto, a former Cambridge University genetics professor, said nothing whatever happened when he hooked a series of plants to a polygraph.

"The pen just traced a flat line," he said.

Some researchers reported that they did get tracings on the graph, but these proved to correspond to changes in humidity in the lab. Is it possible that this is all Backster was measuring?

The man who started the controversy suggests that he has cleared up the mystery of the "green thumb."

If you love your plant, says Cleve Backster, it loves you back and grows better to prove it.

10. The Mystery Deaths of the Caribou

This earth has many nooks and crannies into which are tucked mysteries that defy rational explanation.

Such as this one.

In late June, 1972, a United States military patrol from Fort Greeley, Alaska, explored a small, isolated valley about four miles south of the Greeley Indian reservation. They stumbled on an extraordinary find.

In the isolated valley were 53 dead Alaska caribou. Dead caribou are not in themselves mysterious, but in this case the cause and manner of death were.

The caribou were lying in a circle no more than 50 yards in diameter. Most of the carcasses were within 10 feet of each other. There were 48 adult caribou—most of them females—and five calves.

And there was no visible mark on any of them.

What, then, had killed them?

With investigation, the mystery deepened.

Ken Neiland, a wildlife disease specialist with the Alaska Department of Fish and Game, ruled out disease as the cause of death. The reason: Death had overtaken the animals too suddenly.

They appeared to have dropped in their tracks—all 53 of them. Disease doesn't kill that way.

What's left? Lightning?

That was ruled out because the carcasses showed no burnt hair, and the surrounding terrain was unscorched. If lightning had struck with sufficient power to kill a herd of caribou, it would have left some trace on the nearby grass and other vegetation.

Were the animals shot?

The answer proved to be no. There were no detectable wounds on the caribou. Nor were there any bullet marks on the numerous rocks in the area, though if someone had sprayed hot lead around, some of it would have ricocheted off the surrounding rocks.

Interestingly, several other bands of caribou in the same area were healthy and undisturbed.

Whatever had wiped out the herd had, then, certain characteristics.

1. It killed them suddenly and apparently simultaneously.
2. It left no scars or marks of violence.
3. It evidently could not be described as natural causes.

What's left?

The Alaskan wildlife expert who made the on-the-spot investigation suggested: "The only thing I can imagine doing something like this would be some kind of super-aircraft strafing."

But the aircraft, if such it was, must have used weapons unlike any we know of—weapons that leave no mark on the victim. A death ray, perhaps?

Why and how the caribou perished in that out-of-the-way Alaskan valley remains part of the unexplained . . .

11. "Seeing" with the Fingertips

Scientists are studying a new phenomenon called, variously, extraocular vision, dermooptic vision, and fingertip sight.

This is the apparent ability of some people to distinguish colors, and even to read print, through their fingertips. They appear to "see" through their skin.

In test cases, the subject has been blindfolded, or the objects to be "read" have been hidden inside a container into which the subject placed his hand.

In 1963, the first report on fingertip vision came out of Russia. It said that a girl named Rosa Kuleshova could distinguish colors not only through her fingertips but also through her elbow!

Moreover, it was claimed that Ms. Kuleshova speedily had graduated from perceiving color to reading printed words.

The Russian report was received by Western scientists with about as much enthusiasm as a flu epidemic. Nobody believed it. There was talk that the Russians had been duped, that the girl no doubt was using the standard sideshow trick of peeking down the side of her nose under her blindfold.

However, then came the investigations of Dr. Richard Youtz, a psychology professor at New York's Barnard College, who claimed that a housewife in Flint, Michigan, Mrs. Patricia Stanley, was able to distinguish colors through her fingers.

In tests, said Dr. Youtz, Mrs. Stanley gave the colors of objects correctly between 85 and 90 percent of the time:

"This," the psychologist said, "could occur by chance only once in several million times."

From other tests Dr. Youtz concluded that between 5 and 15 percent of his college students seemed to be able, after practice, to discriminate between different-colored objects. To offset criticisms that a blindfold wasn't an adequate safeguard against peeking, the psychologist used stricter controls.

Around the subject's neck was tied a bib made of black cloth. The other end of the bib was attached to a plywood screen which came down to a few inches from the table top. To touch the test objects, the subject had to thrust his hands under this screen.

Is extraocular vision a nonphysical or a physical phenomenon? In other words, is it a form of ESP or is it something like hyperacute hearing?

Some scientists favor a physical explanation. One theory is that human beings—some, perhaps all—possess "receptors" in the skin of their fingertips, and possibly elsewhere on the body, which pick up some radiation given off by colors. Differences in the radiations from different colors make discrimination possible.

However, would this account for the alleged ability of some subjects to read *words* with their skin as fluently as with their eyes?

The fundamental question of whether the whole phenomenon is real or just a hoax was settled by the discovery of totally blind persons with fingertip vision.

At an international parapsychology conference in Amsterdam in August, 1972, medical psychologist Thelma Moss of the University of California Neuropsychiatric Center in Los Angeles introduced a blind subject said to have extraocular sight.

Mary Wimberley of Los Angeles has one plastic eye, and the optic nerve in the other eye has been severed. However, when objects of different colors are presented to her she was able, by running her fingers over them, to identify the color of each.

Most of the psychologists at the conference tested the subject and got satisfactory results, but one failed to get such results. This suggests that fingertip vision, like ESP, may be influenced by the attitudes and moods not only of the subject but of the experimenter.

Significantly, Dr. Youtz also found that in some of his tests with Mrs. Stanley, her results fell from 85 percent accuracy to 45 percent. He was inclined to attribute the drop to "stagefright."

12. The "Alligator" Insect

Deep in the Amazon jungles lives one of nature's strangest unexplained oddities—an insect that has disguised itself as an alligator.

The purpose of the insect's weird masquerade is to frighten off predatory birds which have learned to have a healthy respect for alligators.

The curious creature is known by the formidable Latin name *Laternaria servillei*. It belongs to the family called lantern-flies.

This particular type of lantern-fly looks exactly like a miniaturized alligator. It has developed a grossly enlarged front portion of the head which resembles an alligator's snout. There are false—that is, nonfunctional—large eyes behind the phony nasal prominence. There is even a partly opened pseudo-mouth, complete with white false teeth.

The lantern-fly looks, for all the world, as though it had enjoyed the services of some ingenious makeup artist. The insect's disguise is accurate even to such a detail as a white mark in the false eyes which simulates the light reflected from a real eye.

Someone may object that surely the lantern-fly's disguise would not fool a bird because of the enormous difference in size between insect and alligator. However birds, it seems, have very poor judgment of size, and are mainly influenced by an object's color and shape.

Therefore, the birds who ordinarily would prey on the lantern-fly apparently do mistake it for an alligator and are scared off.

How did the lantern-fly come to acquire so effective a disguise?

The astonishing resemblance could not be merely chance. The alligator-like features obviously serve purely as a protective mechanism. The false snout, eyes, and mouth have no actual function.

But who told the lantern-fly to masquerade as an alligator?

To account for such a phenomenon, some observers glibly

invoke the name of Darwin and repeat the magic words "evolution" and "natural selection." But these words do not explain how an insect deliberately, as it were, assumes the guise of the creature in its environment which is most feared by the insect's natural enemy.

A British scientist, Dr. Stephen Black, suggests that nature is pervaded by an "information field"—a sort of impersonal super-mind from which living creatures pick up information vital to their survival.

In this theory the lantern-fly "learned" from this super-mind that its best defense against preying birds was to make itself look like an alligator. Then the insect proceeded to do the job, using materials in its outer covering to create the needed disguise.

If evolution, however, is not mindless but guided, who is doing the guiding?

13. Biological Clocks

There are certain tropical worms, called palolos, which live in coral rock and emerge only twice a year. Astonishingly, they always come out on the first day in the months of October and November, when the moon enters the last quarter. Their timing is so precise that the natives of Fiji and Samoa use them as living calendars.

Many scientists say the worms are responding to some "biological clock" attuned to the cosmos around them. And there is growing evidence that probably all living things, including man, respond to similar built-in biological clocks.

In the May, 1967, issue of *Technology Week,* NASA scientists stated that the positions of the planets do influence human behavior. The mechanism of this influence, they indicated, is a resonance between the alpha waves of the human brain and the fundamental pitch of the earth's geomagnetic field, which pulses in accord with changing planetary positions.

Physicist Daniel Cohen in Chicago, measuring the electromagnetic field created by flexing human muscles, reported that it was one five-hundred millionth part as strong as the magnetic field around the earth.

It is known that electromagnetic fields interact, and that a change in a strong field—the earth's geomagnetic field—could predictably be reflected in a change within the lesser field generated by human muscles.

Similarly, biophysicist Robert O. Becker of the State University of New York has noted that each human body has its own electromagnetic field which interacts with the earth's field. He suggests that there is "a general relationship of some kind between the whole of the human species and the whole of the electromagnetic phenomenon that engages the sun, other stars, and the galaxies."

Dr. Becker said that he has established a relationship between the number of admissions to psychiatric hospitals and the earth's magnetic activity, which is profoundly influenced by sun spots. ("Sun spots" are tremendous explosions on the surface of the sun, also called solar flares.)

Apparently sun spots cause changes in the magnetic field around the earth, and these in turn cause changes in the electromagnetic fields surrounding individual humans. These changes could produce jittery nerves or, in the mentally disturbed, violent outbursts.

Two medical researchers studied 28,000 cases of suicide in Europe from 1928 to 1932 and concluded that suicide waves correlated with periods of sun-spot activity.

Dr. Maki Takata, a Japanese medical scientist at Tokyo's Toho University, calls man "a living sundial." He has found that certain characteristic changes in human blood serum relate to solar flares. In other words, the blood in your veins responds to eruptions on the surface of the sun.

Russian medical researchers claim to have found evidence that sun-spot activity bombards the earth with tremendous streams of radiation, which then produce violent changes in the magnetic field around the earth, and that such changes can dramatically affect people's health. Moscow's Institute of Cardiology, in research from 1944 to 1966, discovered a close relationship between heart attacks and such magnetic storms.

These phenomena indicate that man, as a child of the cosmos, is more intimately linked to the stars and the planets than most of us have ever imagined.

14. The Mystery of Anti-Matter

One of the strangest discoveries of science is the existence of anti-matter.

This is a form of matter which is a mirror-like reversal of the stuff of which our earth and the other planets are composed. Anti-matter may form asteroids, planets, stars, or even whole galaxies far out in the abyss of space.

It has not yet been proven that anti-matter actually does exist in nature but the substance has been created by science. Researchers at Brookhaven National Laboratory, Upton, New York, successfully produced particles of anti-matter called anti-deuterons. And since then the mirror-image equivalents of most types of subatomic particles have been similarly created.

This is how Dr. Leon Lederman of Columbia University describes anti-matter: "It is identical to normal matter in most respects but opposite in electrical charge and magnetic characteristics. When matter and anti-matter meet, they destroy each other."

Some scientists speculate that certain great holocausts in history and prehistory may have been caused by chunks of anti-matter colliding with the earth. This might account for such huge holes in the earth as the Chubb Crater in northern Quebec, and for the stupendous explosion near the Tunguska River, Siberia, in June, 1908, which devastated an uninhabited area some 40 miles in diameter.

Nobody really knows what would happen if a sizable mass of anti-matter entered earth's atmosphere from outer space. The force of the resultant explosion might be literally incalculable.

Is it even conceivable that it was a tiny chunk of anti-matter which caused a spectacular celestial phenomenon over Texas on the evening of September 9, 1961?

Thousands of Texans in the Dallas-Fort Worth area were at drive-in theaters when a flash of light blazed in the sky. It was so bright that it momentarily blotted out the picture on the outdoor movie screens.

A local TV station was showing the annual Miss America contest from Atlantic City, when suddenly the television image shattered into innumerable fragments, then coalesced again a moment later. The cause was the same blinding flash in the sky.

Scientist's theorized that a huge meteor had struck the ground somewhere between Dallas and Fort Worth. They searched for the immense crater which would be made by such an impact but none was ever found. What were found were six small meteorite fragments weighing altogether less than a pound.

One of the investigating scientists, Dr. Brian Mason, curator of mineralogy at the American Museum of Natural History, speculated that an enormous meteor streaking toward earth had collided in midair with a chunk of anti-matter and been destroyed.

"The meteorite probably weighed many tons," Dr. Mason was quoted as saying at the time, "but the size of the anti-matter object cannot even be estimated."

He added: "The probability of such a collision before the anti-matter struck the earth was extremely slight—perhaps one in a quadrillion."

If the hypothetical piece of anti-matter had reached the ground, the devastation, Mason estimated, could have equaled that of several Hiroshimas.

There is a way of checking the hypothesis of an anti-matter explosion. When matter and its mirror-image annihilate each other, they produce gamma-rays and particles called kaons and pions. A nuclear reaction then takes place, which releases radiocarbon, an element which is absorbed by living things such as trees.

If trees in the area of an unexplained explosion proved to contain phenomenally large amounts of radiocarbon, this would tend to support the hypothesis that anti-matter was involved in the blast.

Of course, if a big enough chunk of anti-matter hit the earth, there would be no scientists around to analyze what had happened—nor, for that matter, anybody else.

15. Making a Carbon Copy of You

Feats are being done right now in laboratories which the unwary think still belong to science fiction.

For example, duplicating living things—carrots, frogs, maybe even small mammals—as though they were being stamped out with a cookie cutter.

The procedure is called cloning, from the Greek root "to cut."

Many eminent scientists say that some day the method could be used to mass-produce human beings like so many Fords or Chevrolets run off on an assembly line.

Can you imagine a million of you? Or of your mother-in-law? All exact copies of the original?

Admittedly, for the nonscientist this seems as far-out as some of the things you see on the Late Late Show or used to read about in Buck Rogers and Flash Gordon comics. But there isn't much, really, that's comical about it.

In simplest terms, this is what cloning means.

An ordinary body cell from an individual of a species can be stimulated chemically so that it grows into a duplicate of the donor, and the same individual can thus be reproduced hundreds, thousands, even millions of times.

This startling concept was first demonstrated by Professor F. C. Steward of Cornell University. A few years ago he took a lowly carrot, scraped an unfertilized cell from it, and placed the cell in a specially prepared nutrient bath containing, among other things, coconut milk. In this solution the carrot cell began dividing as though it had been pollinated. From a single cell it grew into a mature carrot, roots and all.

Dr. J.B. Gurdon of Oxford University progressed from botanical to biological life. He tried cloning a frog.

Taking an unfertilized egg from a frog, he removed the nucleus.

Then he took an ordinary body cell from another frog—it could be from the intestinal wall or any part of the frog—removed the nucleus, and implanted this nucleus into the egg cell.

This process tricked the egg cell into thinking it was fertilized, and it grew into a complete tadpole, which in turn developed into a frog. This frog was identical—an exact genetic duplicate—to the original donor of the body cell. The cloned frog owed none of its hereditary to the member of its species that provided the egg but everything to the one that donated the body cell.

In other words, the cloned frog had only one parent—and that one could be a male.

Cloning is asexual reproduction. A male could reproduce himself endlessly, a female the same, without need of the other.

Producing a human being by cloning, instead of by the familiar style to which humans have gotten attached, is much more complicated than cloning a frog. But scientists say it will come.

Dr. Kurt Hirschhorn, chief of the division of medical genetics at New York's Mount Sinai School of Medicine, says that cloning will be applied to man "perhaps much sooner than people think." It could be done virtually "right now," he added, if sufficient effort were put forward.

The late Dr. J. H. Muller, a winner of the Nobel Prize in medicine, supported the idea that reproduction of humans by cloning would be scientifically possible in the not remote future.

A man, after all, is different from a frog, but is he all that different? Biologically, I mean.

Whether cloning of human beings is desirable is, of course, another question. Many critics have expressed a preference for reproducing in the old way.

16. A Boy and His Photograph

Does some strange link exist between a person and his photograph?

It sounds like voodoo, but a curious experiment suggests that such a link might actually exist.

The experiment was conducted by an unorthodox British scientist, George de la Warr, at his laboratories in Oxford, England, in August, 1965.

De la Warr based the experiment on the idea that everything in the universe, living and nonliving alike, radiates a form of energy. Radiations are given off even by a photograph, he said, and these provide a link between a person and his picture, no matter how far removed from one another they might be.

On a visit I made to the De la Warr Laboratories, the scientist described to me the experiment with the photograph.

It was set up between De la Warr in Oxford and John Hay, a scientist in Fairfield, Connecticut. Mr. Hay had been sent by De la Warr a photograph of a 17-year-old boy named Rex. The boy himself, in Oxford, was hooked up to a sort of super-polygraph invented by De la Warr to monitor moment-by-moment changes in bodily functioning.

The aim of the experiment was to see if shining a bright light on the boy's photograph in Connecticut coincided with involuntary physical changes in the boy 3,000 miles away.

Watches were synchronized by transatlantic telephone. Then the light was flashed on the boy's photograph in Connecticut for 20 minutes, starting exactly at 4 P.M. British Summer Time or 11 A.M. Eastern Daylight Saving Time.

Details of the experiment were then placed on record, and an affidavit was sworn before a notary public and filed in the state and county of New York.

The results of the experiment?

For the 20-minute period during which the light was directed at his photograph, the boy, on the other side of the Atlantic, showed dramatic involuntary physiological changes as recorded by De la Warr's super-polygraph. George de la Warr's interpretation of these results was: "The shining of the light on the boy's photo apparently triggered energy releases in his body thousands of miles distant."

The skeptic might object: "How do you know that the boy, unconsciously, didn't cause the physiological changes? The changes might have been the result of the power of suggestion."

However, the boy had been kept ignorant of the purpose of the experiment. Unless he was using ESP to find out what was going on (a possibility), it would appear that the involuntary physical changes were indeed correlated in some mysterious way with the light flashing on his photograph across the ocean.

And if this is true, voodoo may not be baloney after all ...

17.   There's an Aura About You

How's my aura?

That's a question you may one day be asking your doctor when you go for a checkup.

He'll tell you—not by listening to your heart or taking your pulse but by snapping your picture.

It's possible that from your photograph, the doctor will be able to deduce not only the present state of your health but, incredibly, what it's likely to be six months in the future.

No, I'm not talking about voodoo but about something called "Kirlian photography," a revolutionary new technique from the Soviet Union, now being investigated by American and Canadian scientists, which captures on film the electrostatic force field, or "aura," around the human body. This aura is said to reflect the individual's physical, mental, and emotional states.

Kirlian machines are usually portable models about the size of a waffle iron (although there is one under construction that will be at least big enough to photograph the whole human body). For now, most Kirlian photographs are of small objects, such as leaves or human fingertips.

These photographs show pulsating, multicolored lights streaming from parts of the human body and from plants, opening up a dazzling and mysterious world hitherto hidden from man's eyes.

An ordinary maple leaf in a Kirlian photograph is surrounded by a galaxy of tiny comets, meteors, flashes, flares, rockets, and twinkling stars. In experiments by Dr. William Tiller, head of the material science department at Stanford University, and medical psychologist Thelma Moss of the University of California at Los Angeles, photographs of freshly plucked leaves showed the light patterns around the leaves intact, but as a leaf slowly died the lights gradually faded.

Also, if the leaf were mutilated, the light patterns around it became distorted.

In human beings, the aura reportedly changes with the individual's moods and physical vitality. Dr. Moss photographed the fingerprints of a medical student before, during, and after the consumption of 17 ounces of whiskey. The lights emitted from his fingertips grew brighter and rosier after every drink until he became "all lit up" and, thereafter, violently sick.

Dr. Gerald Jampolsky, a child psychiatrist in Kentfield, California, told me that he repeated the Moss experiments and achieved the same results.

"When we say a drinker's got a glow on, apparently we are speaking more truly than we realized," remarked Dr. Jampolsky.

The psychiatrist told me he was planning to take Kirlian photographs of the fingertips of children to see if he could determine when a child is daydreaming or actually concentrating on his books.

He is also planning a study of dying patients using Kirlian photographs, the psychiatrist said, to discover how long the aura continues after death, and if the photographs reveal when a patient makes the unconscious decision to stop living and let go.

"Kirlian photographs of people in a hypnotic state show that unconscious decisions—that is, decisions of which the person is not aware at the conscious level—do affect the aura," said Dr. Jampolsky.

It is claimed by some researchers that disease causes characteristic changes in the aura—distortions, dark patches—long before symptoms may be detectable by orthodox medical means.

Cancer, for example, is said to cause a dark blob or shadow to appear in the aura at or near the site of the incipient tumor. Asthma may show up in Kirlian photographs as a smoky, foglike patch in the chest region. Since such changes may occur before any physical signs develop, earlier diagnosis and perhaps cure become possible.

Though this new method of photography was invented more than 30 years ago by the Soviet man-wife team of Semyon and Valentina Kirlian, nobody yet knows exactly what the aura is that it makes so dramatically visible. Some scientists say it is a form of "biomagnetism," while others consider it an electrical "corona" effect, or due to "cold electron emission."

Whatever it is, the aura may play an important part in the science and medicine of the future.

18. Who or What Was Jeff?

There are some things so strange they don't fit into any known category—neither fish nor fowl, human nor nonhuman.

One such thing was Jeff.

The story of this creature is so bizarre that many people will find it impossible to credit. Nevertheless, it is abundantly documented. It was investigated by numerous reporters and psychical researchers, including Dr. Nandor Fodor, a noted psychoanalyst, R.S. Lambert of the British Broadcasting Corporation, and famed ghost-hunter Harry Price.

The story began in the fall of 1931 on the Isle of Man. James T. Irving and his family caught glimpses of a strange animal skulking around their yard. It was described as about the size of a full-grown rat with a flat snout and a small yellow face.

Soon the Irvings became aware that the creature had moved into the house with them. They heard its furtive, rustling movements and found traces of half-eaten food the intruder had pilfered.

Then—and this was a very queer development—the family heard the creature apparently mimicking them in a peculiar imitation of human speech. Over a period of months it acquired the ability to talk in an odd, high-pitched voice. Before long, swore the family, the thing was carrying on conversations with them.

Yes, the story takes some believing thus far. But it gets worse.

The animal, or whatever it was—it never showed itself but lurked in hiding places in the walls from which it conversed with the family—called itself Jeff. It addressed each member of the Irving family by his or her first name. Mr. Irving was "Jim," his wife "Maggie," and their teen-aged daughter "Voirrey."

Jeff, according to the Irvings, did extraordinary things besides talking. They began finding freshly killed rabbits on their kitchen floor—gifts from their mysterious guest. But the rabbits had been strangled, not killed by teeth as a mongoose or weasel (as some thought Jeff to be) would have done. More than 50 rabbits were left in this way.

If the Irvings alone had vouched for Jeff's existence, one might say that it was all a practical joke—or that the whole family was mad. But others encountered Jeff too.

Jeff hated strangers, and when they came to the house to try to make his acquaintance, as many did, he often threw things at them—crockery, or one occasion a large iron bolt.

As time passed, Jeff branched out linguistically and was heard uttering phrases in what appeared to be German and Russian.

R.S. Lambert, a British Broadcasting Corporation producer, spent a week with the Irvings. He went back to London and wrote a book about his experiences with the talking mongoose, or whatever it was. When the book appeared, Lambert's superior publicity branded him either a liar or a madman. Lambert sued in court. The court believed his story and awarded him damages equal to $35,000—a very substantial sum of money in those days.

Other experienced investigators also probed the mystery of Jeff and came away persuaded that he or it represented an insoluble riddle.

Once, on demand, Jeff left his footprints, or pawprints, in several pieces of soft wax and these were pronounced unidentifiable by a zoologist. In other words, they belonged to no known animal.

Jeff stayed with the Irvings four years. Then he vanished—as mysteriously as he had come.

One one occasion, when James Irving demanded to know who or what Jeff really was, the creature, speaking from his usual habitat in the shadows, replied: "I know what I am but I won't tell you. I'm a freak. I've hands and feet. If you saw me you would be petrified."

And then Jeff added these tantalizing words: "I'm a ghost in the form of a weasel . . ."

19. The Ladder of Swords

Nobody knows the biological limits of the human body.

I personally have seen a man, in the presence of medical witnesses, chew up a light bulb and swallow it, stick a sharpened bicycle spoke through one side of his face and out the other, and walk on a fire fed by kerosene—all without serious visible harm.

However, the strange ritual of the Ladder of Swords tops all these.

It is publicly performed every four years in Penang, Malaya. A metal ladder, about 25 feet high, is erected in one of the town squares. There are seventeen rungs in the ladder, each one a steel bar honed to the sharpness of a razor blade. To test this, a spectator gently laid a banana on one of the lower rungs; it was almost sliced in two by its own weight.

When everything is ready, the performers appear. They are male mediums of the Taoist religion, a faith which stresses man's oneness with Nature and Nature's oneness with God.

Before the ceremony begins, the mediums induce a trance by inhaling opium fumes. To try to ascend the Ladder of Swords without putting themselves into trance would have fatal consequences, they insist.

When they are entranced—a state in which, glassy-eyed, they appear oblivious of their surroundings—the mediums one by one climb the Ladder of Swords. Grasping the sword above them with their bare hands, the razor-sharp rungs carrying the full weight of their bodies, they slowly but deliberately climb to the top and then down again.

Astonishingly, none is injured in any way—not even a scratch.

How is it done?

Mass hypnosis? Is the whole ceremony merely a collective hallucination induced in the spectators?

Well, the proceedings have been photographed, even filmed by an American television crew, and cameras are notoriously hard to hypnotize.

The mediums themselves, when asked how they do it, have a simple answer: Perfect faith.

20. The Grieving Foxes
of Ireland

In man's remote, myth-shrouded past, strange ties linked
humans and animals.

Anthropologists know that even today among primitive
peoples a curious relationship may exist between a particular
tribe and a particular kind of animal, usually each tribe having a bond with a different animal.

Called totemism, this peculiar, archaic link between man
and beast lingers on in such things as mascots, or symbols
like the Democratic Party's donkey and the Republican elephant.

In some places totemism still has real power. Among certain tribes around the great Nyanza lakes in central Africa,
such was the power of the totem that should a boat be upset
in crocodile-infested waters, tribesmen who were of the croc-
odile totem were unmolested, while others had to swim for
their lives.

Such a story, bizarre as it sounds, has come from more
than one anthropologist. Geoffrey Gorer, in his book *Africa
Dances* tells of a tribe which possessed an inexplicable link
with the panther and had absolutely no fear of the creature,
though they were normally afraid of the other giant cats.

Gerald Heard, the noted author, philosopher, and at one
time professor of anthropology at Duke University, investigated the strange story of Ireland's grieving foxes of Gormanstown and accepted it as true.

Shortly before the First World War, a prominent Roman
Catholic scholar from England, Abbot Butler of Downside
Abbey, attended the funeral of Lord Gormanstown in Ireland. The Gormanstown title went back to 1478, and the ancestral manor stood on the border of County Meath, not far
from Dublin.

Abbot Butler arrived at the manor the day before the funeral. To his surprise he found the grounds overrun with
what he thought at first were dogs but which he discovered to
be foxes.

The animals behaved in an extraordinary way. Abnormally

quiet and subdued, they showed none of their customary fear of humans.

The foxes—there must have been hundreds of them—seemed almost to be keeping a vigil.

Abbot Butler remarked on their presence to one of the household servants, who frowned, mumbled something unintelligible, and hastily took his leave.

Later, at dinner, the Abbot broached the subject of the foxes to his hostess, Lady Gormanstown, widow of the deceased peer.

She stiffened, went pale, and hurriedly made an excuse to leave the room.

A guest explained to the baffled Abbot:

"I thought everyone knew about the grieving foxes of Gormanstown," he said. "Nobody ever speaks about them in the presence of the family for, as you've seen, it upsets them.

"This is a very ancient family. Whenever a head of the house dies, beginning several hours before the death and until the body is in the ground, all the foxes in the vicinity come to the manor and surround the house.

"I assure you that until the peer is buried, there won't be a fox outside the estate for miles around.

"Of course, why this happens nobody knows."

When Abbot Butler went to his room for the night, he drew back the curtain and saw, in the moonlight, clusters of foxes . . . waiting.

21. The Spinifex Walks

The world is full of monster stories.

The Indians of North America have their tales of Bigfoot, half-man, half-ape. In the Himalayas it's the Yeti, or the Abominable Snowman. In Scotland it's the Loch Ness monster. And in Australia?

Well, in Australia they have the Spinifex—a 10-foot-tall character which, according to aboriginal tribal lore, clubs its human victims to death and then eats them.

Since the summer of 1970, experts in Australia are taking the Spinifex more seriously than they used to. Or at least, they're talking seriously some mysterious footprints which the aborigines claim are the tracks of the fabled monster.

The footprints were first reported in the bush country of Australia, 500 miles northeast of Perth, by Peter Muir, an employee of the Australian Department of Agriculture who knows the aborigines well and is at home in the bush.

The tracks photographed by Muir are extremely curious. They appear to be of a creature with a soft pad and two elongated 10-inch toes on each foot. These apparently were tipped with a claw that kicked back dirt at each stride. The footprints were 15 inches long.

The tracks are unlike those of any known animal. Dr. Basil Marlow, the Australian Museum's expert on mammals, reportedly said: "It is like nothing I have ever seen. What could it be? I'm baffled, utterly baffled by it."

One expert, J.L. Bannister, assistant director of the Western Australian Museum in Perth, said there was a little resemblance to the tracks made by a kangaroo "when it's walking slowly."

Among the more imaginative guesses was the suggestion that the tracks belonged to a deformed camel. This came from Alex Jones, founder of a game preserve in the area where the footprints were found.

"Several types of animals—goats, particularly—suffer from overgrowths on their feet," Mr. Jones remarked. "The same thing has been noticed among camels."

If you're wondering what a camel, deformed or otherwise, is doing in the Australian deserts, it could be a survivor of those used in the past for transportation in the area.

However, Peter Muir, who has spent a lifetime in the bush and knows the tracks of every Australian animal. said the mystery footprints were unlike anything he had seen before.

If we assume for the sake of argument that the tracks were made by an unknown creature, it qualifies as a pretty fair monster. It would appear to be a biped, walking erect, with clawed feet and, judging by the size of the foot, 10 to 15 feet tall.

22.   The Mysterious Silver Thread from Nowhere

Does somebody fish for *us*?

Absurd idea, of course. But what do *you* make of this crazy story?

A silver thread appeared over the house of Mr. and Mrs. A.P. Smith in Caldwell, New Jersey, the first week in August, 1970. It just dangled there, too high to be touched, glinting when the sunlight hit it.

The thread was no illusion. Too many people besides the Smiths saw it—neighbors, police, and various expert witnesses, including Dr. Berthold Schwarz, of Montclair, New Jersey, a psychiatrist interested in strange sightings.

"The thread, so far as any of us could make out, came from no place and went no place," Dr. Schwarz told me recently. "It just hung there.

"Some suggested it must come from a high-rise building, but there was none even remotely close."

Other suggestions were that the thread had been dropped from a blimp—the Goodyear Company blimp was cruising the New York—New Jersey area that summer—or that it was trailing from a runaway kite. However, both these possibilities seemed shot down when the thread remained visible, in the same location, throughout the entire month of August.

On the afternoon of August 31, Mrs. Smith heard "a loud thunderclap, which she attributed to a jet breaking the sound barrier," said Dr. Schwarz. Shortly after, she noticed that the mysterious thread had fallen to the ground.

The substance proved to be nylon fishline. It did not match any of the types available in stores in New Jersey or New York. Stiff and translucent, it was described as looking more like a fiber from a plastic broom than a typical fishline.

The conclusion of the matter?

Dr. Schwarz shrugged.

"The sensible explanation is that the string was some kind of fishing line. But where was it dangling from for a month?"

The psychiatrist said that he put a piece of the substance in an envelope, sealed it, and mailed it to a fellow investigator in another city in New Jersey.

"The envelope arrived," said Dr. Schwarz, "but the specimen of line wasn't in it. Obviously, it either had disintegrated on the way or been removed."

And so the silver thread remains a mystery of the unexplained . . .

23. Weighing the Soul?

How much does a soul weigh?

Yes, it's a crazy question. But some men have tried to find an answer to it.

Recently Dr. Nils-Olof Jacobson, a Swedish physician, cited evidence that the human soul weighs about three-quarters of an ounce.

Dr. Jacobson said the evidence was obtained by placing terminal cancer patients and their beds on highly sensitive scales to record any loss of weight at the moment of death.

With this apparatus, a weight loss of 21 grams—or three-quarters of an ounce—was recorded, he says.

The experiments were reported as long ago as 1906 by Dr. Duncan MacDougall of the Massachusetts General Hospital, Boston.

MacDougall built a light framework on delicately balanced beam-type scales. This framework held a bed on which the patients to be used in the experiment were placed. All the patients were in a dying condition, and all had diseases which terminated in profound exhaustion, so that there was little or no muscular movement to jar the scales.

The scales were sensitive to one-tenth of an ounce.

Dr. MacDougall took into account such factors as the weight to the air exhaled from the patient's lungs and the loss of body fluids. Even with these allowances, however, several patients registered a sudden unaccountable weight loss at what appeared to be the moment of death (although sometimes this is hard to determine precisely).

The inexplicable loss was uniformly three-quarters of an

ounce. Thus, the cited findings by Dr. Jacobson stand as reported more than half a century ago by Dr. MacDougall.

The Boston physician agreed with the conclusion of the Swedish doctor—that at the moment of death something measurable leaves the human body.

But what could it be? Surely an immaterial soul would have no weight?

Well, there is a persistent tradition in the folklore of many cultures that human beings have *two* bodies. The second body is said to be the vehicle of the spirit. Ancient Egyptians called it the "ka" and pictured it in tomb paintings as a bird.

Often dubbed the "psychic double" or the "astral body," this counterpart form is said to be a duplicate of the physical except for blemishes. Composed, so it's said, of an attenuated matter, this second body would be measurable.

Is this what the doctor weighed?

PART II

Mysteries of UFO's

24. Mystery Explosion
over Nevada

Man has walked on the moon, and now Mars beckons. But is it two-way traffic?

The following story is fully documented—the date, time, and place when the events about to be described took place. However, we lack any satisfactory explanation of just what it was that took place.

On April 18, 1962, at approximately 7:30 P.M., an unidentified flying object exploded over Nevada about seventy miles from Las Vegas.

The headline in the *Las Vegas Sun* the next day shouted: BRILLIANT RED EXPLOSION FLARES IN LAS VEGAS SKY.

A secondary headline said: WEIRD OBJECT SEEN THROUGH ENTIRE WEST.

The facts behind these headlines?

Well, some facts are plain. For one thing, the tremendous aerial explosion lit up the evening sky so brightly that it tripped the photoelectric cells which control the street lights in Las Vegas, and the lights went off—as though daylight had arrived at 7 P.M.

Spokesmen at the U.S. Air Defense Command at Colorado Springs, Colorado, told newsmen the following details about the explosion.

A mysterious object, they said, with a trail of fire, streaked over the continental United States on the night of April 18, 1962. It was tracked on radar westward from New York. Thus, it appeared not to be a meteor, said the military authorities, because meteors can't be tracked by radar (although their ionized trails may be).

The Air Defense Command sent up jets from Phoenix, Arizona, to intercept the alarming aerial intruder.

At the time of the incident it was reported that a huge object of unknown identity landed briefly at Eureka, Utah, and a power station was temporarily put out of action by the impact of "the thing." Air Force spokesmen at the time are said to have admitted the landing but refused to give newsmen further details. The strange object reportedly took off again and flashed westward over Nevada.

Then it blew up—with a blaze of light clearly seen a hundred miles away in Reno, and even in California.

The military authorities later revised their original statements. Although they had at first called the object "unidentified," they later announced that it was an experimental guided missile with an atomic warhead sent aloft from Vandenburg Air Force Base. The missile went crazy, said the revised Air Force statement, and ground control had to press the "destruct" button, blowing it up in midair.

The trouble with this story is that Vandenburg Air Force Base is in California, which means a projectile fired from there surely would have been going *east* over Nevada, whereas the mystery object was traveling *west*.

Moreover, isn't it a little hard to believe that the United States Air Force would experiment over its own territory with a missile bearing a live atomic warhead?

Something went bang over Nevada. What was it?

25. The Return of the UFO's

A few ounces of a "white fibrous substance," which seemed to defy scientific analysis, represented possibly the first tangible evidence of the reality of UFO's.

This word came not from a flying-saucer cultist, or some crackpot "contactee" who says he's talked to little green Martians, but from the world's foremost scientific authority on UFO's.

Dr. J. Allen Hynek, chairman of the department of astronomy at Northwestern University, Evanston, Illinois, told me about the mysterious white substance and other physical traces found at the site of an alleged near-landing of a UFO in Delphos, Kansas, last November 2. (The substance later proved to be a chemical precipitate caused by strange changes in the soil produced by the UFO.)

There were three witnesses to the sighting—16-year-old

Ronnie Johnson and his parents. They reported seeing a lumi-
nous object, some eight feet across, swoop down into their
farmyard and hover about two feet above the ground. After
"a few minutes," the object rose into the sky and streaked
away.

The UFO reportedly left behind a strange "glowing ring"
on the ground. When UFO experts reached the site a few
days later, the ring was not glowing but it was clearly visible.
Though the surrounding soil was muddy from heavy rains,
the ring, as an investigating sheriff put it, "was as dry as if it
had been sitting in the desert for ten years."

The ring also was found to contain the mysterious white
substance.

Dr. Hynek told me that extensive tests at four independent
laboratories showed that soil taken from the ring differed
markedly from the surrounding soil. It had an abnormally
high calcium content (up to 10 times that of the earth around
it), would not absorb water as normal soil does, and plants
refused to grow in it, although they grew in the surrounding
soil.

This is just one of the most recent UFO sightings out of
hundreds personally investigated by Dr. Hynek. For 22 years,
he was the official astronomical consultant on UFO's to the
U.S. Air Force. He had access to the files of "Project
Bluebook," the Air Force's UFO investigation program which
was closed out in 1969.

With his background, which makes him the ranking scientific expert on the UFO mystery, Dr. Hynek says: "The evidence strongly suggests empirical observations which
described a new fact—that UFO's exist."

Dr. Hynek summarizes and evaluates this evidence in a
new book, The UFO Experience, published by Henry Reg-
nery Co. In it, besides a mass of eye-witness reports of sightings, there are numerous UFO photographs which Dr. Hynek
feels deserve to be taken seriously.

There is a photo related to a reported UFO landing on an
Iowa farm which was witnessed by the farmer, his teen-aged
daughter, and a teen-aged girl cousin. The UFO left behind "a
parched circle of roughly 40 feet diameter in an otherwise
unmolested large field of soybeans."

(These burned or parched circles, which occur frequently
in UFO landing reports, appear to be caused by some "mi-
cro-wave or shock wave effect," Dr. Hynek says.)

There are cases in which UFO's have been sighted simultaneously on radar and visually. Hynek quotes the account of an Anglican priest who described a huge, disk-shaped, silvery object with "humanoids" on its outside deck which was seen for several minutes by "a great many" witnesses.

There is case after case in which pilots, policemen, military personnel, even astronomers report seeing UFO's under conditions that appeared to leave little room for misobservation.

What are UFO's? Where do they come from?

These questions, in Dr. Hynek's judgment, are premature. What's needed, he says, is a think-tank of top scientists to try to come to grips with the mystery.

"There is," he said, "a growing 'Invisible College' of scientifically and technically trained persons who are intrigued by the UFO phenomenon.

"They represent an international group ready to accept the tremendous challenge of the UFO."

26. Science Tackles UFO's

So you thought UFO's were things seen only by drunks or people who needed new glasses?

Wrong. So far wrong, in fact, that a group of scientists have opened a Center for UFO Studies to tackle what they consider to be one of the deepest and most important mysteries facing science.

"The time is definitely past when anybody could say that UFO's are all nonsense," declared the center's director, Dr. J. Allen Hynek.

In an interview, Dr. Hynek told me that associated with him at the UFO center is an "invisible college" of scientists from such universities as Stanford, Chicago, Johns Hopkins, Colorado, and UCLA, representing a range of disciplines—astronomy, physics, engineering, biology, medicine, statistics, and sociology.

And what is it, exactly, that they are studying?

That, said Dr. Hynek, is the mystery.

"We don't know what the UFO phenomenon represents," he admitted, "but we know it's real."

How about spaceships from another planet?

"Personally," said Dr. Hynek, "the more I study the evidence, the further away I get from any idea of nuts-and-bolts hardware from outer space. The UFO's are just too puzzling, too bizarre for that theory."

What are they, then? Or what could they be?

"Publicly, I'm only prepared to go this far," said Dr. Hynek. "The evidence shows that there is some form of intelligence behind the UFO phenomenon. The activities of UFO's are not random. But beyond that . . ."

He shrugged.

Off the record, some scientific ufologists are prepared to speculate that UFO's may be intrusions from a parallel universe—another world or dimension occupying the same space as the one we live in and yet not interacting with our world because of differences in the structure of its matter.

How would such transdimensional visitors get from there to here?

Possibly through the mysterious "black holes" in space which, according to some scientific ufologists, may actually be openings or corridors into another dimension.

All such speculation is, of course, just that—speculation. But the Center for UFO Studies is solid fact.

Dr. Hynek said the center has five main purposes: (1) to serve as a clearing house to which persons can report UFO experiences without fear of ridicule or unwanted publicity, and with the knowledge that their reports will receive serious attention; (2) to mount an all-out scientific assault on UFO's; (3) to provide bulletins and technical UFO data to universities, scientific organizations, and the general public; (4) to help coordinate a worldwide UFO study; and (5) to synthesize the insights of various scientific disciplines.

The Center for UFO Studies has a mailing address—P.O. Box 11, Northfield, Illinois 60093. And it also operates a toll-free hot line (the number available only to police departments, planetariums, and similar agencies) to receive UFO reports.

In one week, March 23-30, 1974, the Center received UFO reports from 22 police departments in such places as Valparaiso, Indiana; Berwyn, Pennsylvania; Wayland, Massachusetts; Bangor, Maine; Portsmouth, New Hampshire; Blude Jacket, Oklahoma; Alhambra, California; and Los Angeles.

The reports include cases in which UFO's were sighted at treetop level; in which way they landed and left behind a "burned ring" 40 feet in diameter; in which they buzzed police cruisers, temporarily stalling the motor; and in which they approached military and commercial aircraft on a collision course, veering away at the last possible moment.

"The UFO mystery," says Dr. Hynek, "is the greatest challenge science has today."

27. A Visitor from Outer Space

The Pioneer 10 spacecraft streaking through space toward Jupiter, and the stars beyond, carries a plaque designed to inform any extraterrestrial intelligence which may intercept the rocket as to where it came from and what sort of beings launched it.

Which raises the question: Has extraterrestrial intelligence already made contact with earth?

Ten years ago, this question might have been considered crazy but today authorities such as Carl Sagan, the young astrophysicist at Cornell University who designed the Pioneer 10 plaque, take it seriously.

In conversation with Dr. Sagan, he reaffirmed his hypothesis that in the distant past our earth may have received space visitors.

Scientists in the Soviet Union believe that evidence of such a space visitor in very recent times exists in Siberia. But the identity of the visitor is shrouded in mystery.

The mystery sprouted at exactly 7:17 A.M., June 30, 1908.

A huge ball of fire shot across the sky over Siberia. Travelers on the Trans-Siberian Railroad observed the incandescent mass moving at a fantastic speed from north to south. Suddenly there was a stupendous explosion.

It is hard to appreciate the immensity of the blast. Seismographs around the world registered an earth tremor. One seismograph more than 500 miles from the center of the explosion didn't stop quivering for almost an hour.

The noise of the cataclysm was heard 600 miles away. Whole herds of reindeer were incinerated, and trees were uprooted over a wide area.

What caused the awesome upheaval?

Presumably something from outer space collided with the

earth. In the absence of concrete data, the object was assumed to have been a meteorite and for years was referred to as the Tunguska Meteorite.

But was it a meteorite?

In 1927, almost 20 years after the mystery explosion, an official Russian scientific team was sent to Siberia to conduct an on-the-spot study. The scientists found some puzzling things.

The scene of the blast, nearly three decades later, was still scorched and barren. Trees had been snapped off like matchsticks as far as 37 miles from the center of the explosion.

To test the meteor theory, the Russians combed the site for meteor fragments. They found none, though in their search they drilled into the earth to a depth of 118 feet.

Well if the object was not a meteorite, what was it? Nobody, in 1927, had a theory to fit the curious facts of the case.

However, nearly 20 years later, one of the scientists on that team, Dr. Alexander Kazentsev, was among a group of Soviet experts who went to Hiroshima to study the effects of the atom bomb which had obliterated that Japanese city. Dr. Kazentsev was struck by the remarkable similarity between the kind of devastation in Hiroshima and that left by the mysterious explosion in Tunguska, Siberia.

In 1963 Dr. Kazentsev was part of another scientific team which visited the site of the blast. This time, he and most of his colleagues concluded that the explosion more than 50 years earlier was nuclear in nature. Further, on the basis of their calculations they agreed that the explosion had been triggered by some sort of nuclear-powered object more than half as big as an ocean liner.

Moreover, the consensus among the scientists was that the object blew up in midair more than a mile above the earth. Dr. Kazentsev called the object a spaceship.

In an official report to the Soviet government he summed up the results of the investigation this way:

"The thing which was long known as the Tunguska meteorite was in reality some very large artificial construction, weighing in excess of 50,000 tons, which was being directed toward a landing when its atomic engines exploded. . . ."

28. The Missionary and the UFO

From time to time there have been reports of UFO's involving living creatures.

No, they usually aren't described as little green men but as "humanoid" beings.

Some of these reports invite skepticism coming, as they do, from people who need their glasses fixed or partygoers on the way home after an evening of excessive libations.

But some of the reports originate with sober observers, such as policemen, on-duty pilots and radar personnel, and clergymen.

And the scientist who knows more about UFO's than any other single person, Dr. J. Allen Hynek, thinks that some of the reports of "humanoids" deserve to be taken very seriously.

"My conclusion," Dr. Hynek told me, "is that after considering all known conventional explanations, twenty percent of UFO sightings remain unexplained."

Some of the most impressive sightings involve humanoids, he added, citing a case which has "profoundly impressed" him.

The incident, said Dr. Hynek, occurred on the evening of June 26, 1959, in New Guinea. The principal witness was an Anglican priest, the Reverend William Bruce Gill, whose account was supported by more than 30 parishioners who evidently saw what he saw.

This is how Father Gill described what he saw:

"We watched this sparkling, very bright disk in the sky and what appeared to be human beings on it.

"The object, which may have been as big as a large house, had what seemed to be a deck on top of the disk. There were four figures on it in all.

"One of the men seemed to lean over, as though over a rail, and look down on us, and I waved one hand overhead. The figure did the same, as though in response.

"Some of my companions also waved and the four figures on the strange craft seemed to wave back.

"The object at one point came quite close to the ground and we thought it was going to land. But unfortunately it did not . . ."

In his account, Father Gill took care to note that throughout the sighting the planet Venus was clearly visible elsewhere in the sky, ruling out the theory, always advanced by some skeptic, that the UFO was really Venus.

This careful account by a sober, responsible witness leaves unanswered the question: What did Father Gill and his companions see? Dr. Hynek says that conventional science has no answer.

29. Is Another World Watching?

Is the earth at this moment orbited by a space probe from an extraterrestrial civilization?

The idea, outlandish as it sounds, is being taken seriously by a respected body of British scientists who plan to investigate the possibility that our planet is being monitored by a satellite from who-knows-where.

In 1968, a distinguished American astronomer, Professor R. N. Bracewell of Stanford University, speculated that one method by which an alien civilization in space might try to contact us would be by putting an unmanned probe in orbit around the earth. Such a probe probably would be programmed to transmit to earth a picture, he suggested, rather than words in a language we couldn't understand. And a logical choice for such a picture would be a map of the sky as astronomers know it.

And now, a Scottish amateur astronomer, Duncan Lunan, has come up with provocative data suggesting that such a space probe may actually be in orbit around our planet.

Lunan, the 27-year-old president of the Scottish Association for Technology and Research in Astronautics, was interested in reports of curious echoes from space which had been picked up by radio researchers since the 1920's. Some researchers said they found that when they sent out a series of pulses they received two sets of echoes, the second set 3 to 15 seconds after the first.

One set of echoes clearly was bouncing off what's called the ionosphere, a radiation belt high above the earth in roughly the same orbit as the moon.

As Lunan studied these second echoes it occurred to him that possibly the variation in delay times formed some kind of intelligent signal. In other words, maybe the object, whatever it was, transmitted signals of its own besides returning the radio pulses from earth.

Lunan detected a peculiar pattern in the signals. Translating them into lines on graph paper, he came up with an astounding result—a recognizable map of the various star constellations. The hypothetical object circling the earth was transmitting a map of the sky.

Moreover, Lunan discovered that all the reference lines in the star map seemed to converge on a single point, identified as a star known as Epsilon Bootes, which is 103 light years from earth. Could this be the source of the mystery object?

Is Duncan Lunan letting his imagination run away with him? Is the resemblance of his graphs to an actual star map merely a curious coincidence?

Most scientists who've examined the case say yes. But a British computer expert, Antony Lawton, said that the odds against Lunan's star map being the product of chance alone are 10,000 to one.

At any rate, the British Interplanetary Society is going to look into the matter.

Meanwhile, I wonder what intelligent beings on another planet would make of our television commercials?

30. The Policeman and the UFO

Reports of UFO's piloted by little men (green or otherwise) have a low credibility.

However, a distinguished scientist told me about such a case which he considers impressive enough to be taken very seriously.

The incident happened on April 24, 1964, but is little known outside the small world of ufologists. The scientist who took a fresh look at the case, including interviewing the persons involved, was Dr. James McDonald, senior physicist in the Institute of Atmospheric Physics, University of Arizona.

The UFO sighting involved Police Sergeant Lonnie Zamora who was on patrol in Socorro, New Mexico. Suddenly he was startled by a loud roar that sounded like an explosion. Zamora pulled his cruiser over to the curb and got out to investigate.

Peering into a deep gully, he saw what appeared at first to be an overturned automobile. He returned to the cruiser and radioed that he was checking out a possible wreck.

But on looking again, Sergeant Zamora realized that the object in the gully wasn't a car. What in the world was it?

Lonnie Zamora said later he had never seen anything like it. The object appeared to be a craft of some sort. It was weird-looking—an egg-shaped cylinder about 15 feet long and resting on four metal legs.

However, what the policeman saw beside the object was even more unsettling. Two humanlike figures, about three feet high and wearing silvery coveralls and bubble helmets, apparently were scooping up samples of soil and rock into a container. They seemed unaware of Zamora's presence.

Suddenly the humanoids noticed him. They scampered up a ladder into the object, Zamora said. The officer, by this time emotionally shaken, rushed back to his cruiser and radioed for help.

At that moment another cruiser pulled up, driven by Sergeant Sam Chavez who was responding to Zamora's earlier call about a car wreck. Zamora was babbling out his story to Chavez when both officers heard a roar, saw a bright blue streak, and a white object hurtled overhead at enormous speed, vanishing in the distance in seconds.

The two policemen immediately investigated the gully. They found charred and smoking bushes and four deep indentations in the soil, presumably made by the object's landing gear.

Later, the United States Army investigated the site carefully and cross-examined both police officers. To this day, no plausible explanation of the strange object, or its reported diminutive occupants, has been offered.

31. The Mystery of the USO's

UFO, of course, stands for Unidentified Flying Object—but have you heard of the USO?

That's an Unidentified Submerged Object.

There are many reports, some well documented, of strange, unclassifiable objects prowling not the sky above but the seas and oceans. Consider these typical cases.

On August 29, 1964 the U. S. oceanographic ship *Eltanin* was taking pictures with an underwater camera at 13,500 feet below the surface some 1,000 miles west of Cape Horn.

One of the photographs captured what looked like a curious piece of machinery on the ocean floor, with projecting rods that could have been antennae. It seems inconceivable that this was a plant, since no sun reaches those abysmal ocean depths. The only other natural explanation that seems conceivable is that it was an unknown type of coral.

The notion of a machine, evidently not man-made, at the bottom of the sea may sound bizarre. But what was it that the noted oceanographer, Dr. Dmitri Rebikoff, saw and attempted to photograph in the Gulf Stream on July 5, 1965? It was "a huge pear-shaped object," he said, and definitely no form of aquatic life with which he, with all his marine experience, was familiar.

And what about this account, with 40 eyewitnesses to vouch for it, of an unclassifiable something that intercepted the Argentine cargo ship *Naviero* at midnight on July 30, 1967.

The object, spotted off the coast of Brazil, was "the shape of a Cuban cigar and glowed with a strange green, almost white phosphorescence." That's how Captain Juliana Ardanza, skipper of the vessel, described the eerily shimmering USO.

"It was an object which navigated and submerged, as any submarine, but its strange luminosity made it unusual," he continued. "It was not a mirage or illusion but a real thing."

More recently, something unidentifiable invaded the waters of Northern Europe.

On November 23, 1972, the story hit the news wire that

for two weeks the Norwegian navy, aided and abetted by the British, had been playing catch-me-if-you-can with what they thought was an unknown submarine. The intruder was in the Sogne Fjord, north of Bergen.

There were reports of a "yellowish-green spotlight" on the fjord and sightings of a dark object on the surface for about seven minutes. One night six red rocket flares were seen in the fjord. Observers said the flares "appeared to come straight out of the sea." The Norwegian navy dropped anti-submarine bombs with no result.

Strangely enough, at times the Norwegian and British military communications frequencies used for the sub hunt were jammed by some unknown agency.

The extraordinary thing is that this massive Norwegian-British anti-submarine operation, using every available sophisticated technique, was unable even to establish whether there was indeed something down there, though there was no doubt of it.

Norwegian radio carried a report that the country's Defense Command did not believe the intruder was a foreign submarine and labeled it simply "an unidentified submerged object."

And that's the way the mystery still stands. The whole flap ended when the thing, whatever it was, vanished from the fjord.

Well, it must have been a submarine, you may say, probably nuclear-powered. Fair enough. But what, then, about this well-documented account, which goes back to the pre-modern submarine era.

According to the log of the British steamship *Fort Salisbury*, the second officer, Mr. A. H. Raymer, on October 28, 1902, at 3:05 A.M., in Latitude 5 degrees 31 S. and Longitude 4 degrees 32 W., saw, with the lookout, "a huge dark object bearing lights in the sea ahead.

"Two lights were seen as the steamship passed a slowly sinking bulk of an estimated length of 500 or 600 feet. Mechanism of some kind was making a commotion in the water . . ."

We can add to the world of the unexplained, the USO.

PART III

Mysteries of Faith and Healing

32. The Healer Doctors Believe In

Olga Worrall is a faith healer even doctors believe in.

In a recent issue of the respected publication *Medical Economics,* this grandmotherly Baltimore woman who has been practicing spiritual healing, as she calls it, for 40 years, was praised by several physicians.

Said Dr. Robert Bradley, a Denver gynecologist: "I've known of Olga Worrall over a number of years and I've come to the conclusion that she's a sincere person with a decided gift for healing."

Dr. Paul G. Isaak, a family physician in Alaska, remarked of Mrs. Worrall as a healer: "I must say I am favorably impressed."

Dr. William McGary, director of an Arizona clinic, commented: "Olga Worrall has a remarkable ability to heal."

And Dr. James A. Knight, associate dean and professor of psychiatry at the Tulane University medical school, said: "I view Mrs. Worrall's healing ministry with enthusiasm and confidence."

And what does the chatty, 67-year-old healer, who calls everybody "honey," have to say for herself?

"Don't call me a miracle worker," she says. "I simply channel to the afflicted a primal healing power that flows from God. God is the healer, not me. So-called miracles are the working out of the laws of God on a higher level than we understand."

Mrs. Worrall, who accepts no money for her healing work, has conducted faith-healing services for many years at Baltimore's Mount Washington Methodist Church. She is the widow of an aeronautical engineer who had a reputation as a healer in his own right. Ambrose Worrall went everywhere with his wife as half of a healing team. Since his death in 1972 she still signs her letters to friends with "Ambrose and Olga."

What sort of cases respond to Olga Worrall's brand of spiritual therapy?

Gail Washington, whose mother runs a Baltimore nursing home, was born with severe brain damage; by the age of four she was deaf, blind, and suffering from a serious heart condition. Her brain was so extensively destroyed that doctors described her head as almost empty.

Mrs. Washington took her daughter to an Olga Worrall healing service—not once but many, many times over a period of several years. The child gradually improved to the point where today she's described as a virtually normal schoolgirl.

Coincidence? A freak remission of symptoms? Or the delayed result of medical treatment?

Well, a doctor who knew the case well said he did not believe "that medical treatment alone could have saved the girl."

In another case, a Baltimore boy, Jeffrey Kenney, suffered from a crippling bone disease that doctors said would disable him permanently. Mrs. James Kenney took her son to Olga Worrall, and today the boy no longer wears his leg brace and appears perfectly normal.

Of this case, a doctor said cautiously: "Recovery did occur where medically it was not logically expected to occur." But, he added, the cure may have been the result of "sheer will-power" on the boy's part.

Olga Worrall says she isn't fussy who gets the credit as long as a sick person gets well. She has excellent relations with doctors and always encourages people who come for healing to continue their medical treatment until such time as it becomes obvious they no longer need it.

Thus, she avoids the dangerous practice, for which some faith healers are criticized by the medical profession, of encouraging or even exhorting people to throw away their medications and simply "have faith." Because of her pro-medical approach, Olga Worrall frequently finds doctors among those who come to her for healing prayer.

"One night," she recalls with a chuckle (she often chuckles), "there were nine M.D.'s in the house, all seeking spiritual therapy for their own ailments."

In a field that's riddled with fraud, fantasy, and dangerous extremism, Olga Worrall comes on like sanity itself—cool, soft-spoken, reasonable, yet compassionate.

"The thing that permitted miracles to happen 2,000 years ago is still around," she says so calmly that it's hard not to believe her, "if only we would make use of it."

33. An Eye Is Healed by Faith

Faith may help, nearly everybody would agree, if you've got a nervous stomach but what can it do for a broken arm or a punctured eye?

The typical doctor would say not much. Faith, so the accepted notion goes, is fine for illness caused by nerves or imagination but not for something real.

However, a growing body of evidence, much of it amassed by doctors themselves, indicates that faith or prayer may be far more powerful than most of us have thought possible.

For example, what about a case of a serious eye lesion healed by faith?

The case comes from the files of Dr. Clair King, Canton, Ohio, an ophthalmologist who has a joint practice with his son, also an eye specialist.

On August 29, 1953, a four-and-a-half-year-old boy was brought to Dr. King for treatment of an eye injury.

"The boy had been hit in the eye by a piece of flying glass," Dr. King told me in an interview. "He had a large through-and-through laceration of the cornea with a prolapse of the iris."

In layman's terms, this means that the cornea, the window of the eye that lets light in and makes vision possible at all, had a hole in it, and sticking out of the hole was a piece of the iris, the pulpy colored part of the eye that lies behind the cornea.

"It was a serious wound," Dr. King said. "We operated right away to repair the damage. The procedure was to cut off the protruding part of the iris and pull a flap of conjunctiva, the thin, glasslike membrane that covers the white of the eye, over the wound for it to heal."

The eye seemed to be healing nicely until September 8, a little over a week later, when pressure inside the eye caused the wound to split open. The iris was once more sticking out of the wound.

"We decided to operate again to repeat the procedure of repairing the wound," said Dr. King, "but that operation never took place."

What happened?

"Well," he said, looking up from his case files, "that's the point of the story.

"You see, the boy was admitted to the hospital for the scheduled surgery. But when we—my son and I—saw him in the operating room, the wound in his eye was perfectly healed. My notation on the record is, 'No operation necessary!' "

Dr. King said he and his son were surprised and puzzled by the strange turn of events. *Something* had happened to the boy, but what?

Later, Dr. King found out.

"Between the time we examined the boy and the date of the scheduled second operation, his mother had taken him to a miracle service led by evangelist Kathryn Kuhlman in Youngstown, and asked for prayer for the boy's healing.

"Later, when I saw Miss Kuhlman, I joked with her about the case and said, 'You cheated us out of an operation!' "

Wouldn't such an eye injury have healed itself, I asked Dr. King, with or without prayer? Wasn't it possible that the hole in the boy's cornea just closed up on its own?

"Well, I've never seen it happen," he said, "and I've seen hundreds of such lesions of the eye. They don't heal themselves. Let me put it this way: I just don't think it's medically possible.

"You see, in this case the iris was sticking out through the wound and as long as that iris was in there, the wound wouldn't heal. It would be like sticking a piece of cloth into a wound; the edges of tissue wouldn't come together and you couldn't get it to heal.

"I've never heard of another single case where a prolapsed iris went back into place and the perforation of the cornea healed."

Since this experience, Dr. King said, he has become a believer in prayer and faith as valuable additions to medical therapy.

34. Prayers and Pills

An increasing number of doctors are saying that prayers as well as pills can play a part in healing.

One of them is Dr. Platon Collipp, chief of pediatrics at the Nassau County Medical Center in New York. He says that a recent study of his own supports the view that prayer makes a difference.

He set up an experiment using two groups of young people with acute leukemia, the cancerlike disease of the blood. One, made up of 10 patients, served as the experimental group; the other, with eight patients, was the control group.

The names of the first group were given to 10 families in a prayer circle composed of the doctor's friends. Each family received the name of one leukemia patient for whom they were to pray daily over a 15-month period.

The control group received no such prayers.

To rule out the possibility of suggestion, Dr. Collipp didn't tell any of the leukemia patients that they were being prayed for.

(It is a known medical fact, you see, that as many as 40 percent of patients will improve after receiving a "placebo"—a dummy pull that they think is a potent medicine.)

The results of the study?

Of the 10 patients who received daily prayer, seven were still alive after 15 months. Of the eight who were not prayed for, only two were alive after the same period.

A statistical analysis of these results, according to Dr. Collipp, indicated that there was a 90 percent chance the difference between the two groups was due to prayer, or only a 10 percent chance that it was coincidence.

Not all doctors are convinced. Some medical critics have faulted Dr. Collipp's scientific method, his statistics, or both.

However, he says, "My final opinion is that the results support the view that prayer is efficacious."

Further support for this view comes from another doctor

who claims to have had unusual success treating cancer by a combination of medicine and meditation.

Meditation can be interpreted as a form of "higher prayer" in which the person tries to attune himself to God, the Cosmic Mind, or however he conceives the ultimate reality.

Dr. O. Carl Simonton, an Air Force major who's chief of radiation therapy at California's Travis Air Force Base, teaches his cancer patients to put themselves into meditation, a deeply relaxed state of mind, and then "talk to" their body, ordering it to kill the cancer and return to normal health.

Three times a day the patient is supposed to meditate and visualize himself well and strong. All the while he continues to receive standard medical treatment from Dr. Simonton.

In some cases, says the doctor, this combination of medicine and meditation brings results which medicine alone couldn't have produced. He doesn't use the word "cure"—it's too soon for that. He uses the word "remission"— a disappearance of symptoms, how permanent only time will tell.

In one case, a 61-year-old man with advanced cancer of the throat was given only a five percent chance of survival. He received radiation therapy and also meditated regularly, visualizing himself as well and strong.

Today, two years later, contrary to the medical prognosis, he's doing fine and appears cancer-free.

Dr. Simonton's view is that cancer is basically due to a breakdown in the body's own immunological defense system. Such a breakdown he suggests, may be traced to negative states of mind—deep despair, hopelessness, or a death wish.

Revive the will to live, to fight back, he says, and wonderful things can follow.

35. Is This the Face of Christ?

Preserved in the chapel of the cathedral in Turin, Italy, is a relic venerated by millions of Roman Catholics, and some Christians of other churches, as a direct link with Jesus Christ.

Called the Shroud of Turin, it is a piece of linen, about 15 feet long and 4 feet wide, blotched by numerous scorch marks and water stains, the result of a fire which almost destroyed it in 1532.

The cloth also bears the mysterious image of a man's nude body—the body of a victim of crucifixion, with wounds in the hands, feet, and brow, and one in the region of the heart.

The church does not require belief in the Shroud. In fact, numerous Catholic critics—notably the British Jesuit, Herbert Thurston—declared it a pious fraud. The believers—and these include agnostic scientists—consider it to be the actual burial sheet of Christ. And the image on it, they submit, is no mere painting but the very likeness of Christ.

The man on the Shroud is just a fraction of an inch under six feet tall. He has shoulder-length hair parted in the middle, and a full beard. His face, in the repose of death, is serene, dignified, even majestic. Distilled into it is all the sorrow of the ages.

Is the Shroud really the winding sheet of Christ?

Here is a summary of the historical, medical, and scientific data bearing on that question.

Early historical allusions to a shroud of Christ are scanty. Though such references go back at least to the sixth century, and several historians mention a shroud being exhibited in Constantinople in the twelfth and thirteenth centuries, the first indisputable allusion to what is now the Shroud of Turin was in 1353.

At that time the relic turned up in Troyes, France. In 1481 it passed into the safekeeping of the House of Savoy which, upon becoming Italy's ruling dynasty, placed the relic in the Turin cathedral where it now rests.

The medical and scientific data about the Shroud are more interesting.

Scientific study has been almost fatally hampered by the church's refusal to allow chemical analysis of the stains on the fabric, or dating by the Carbon-14 method, on the grounds that the relic might be damaged. However, indirect examination of the Shroud is possible by photography.

The first photographs of the Shroud, taken in 1898, revealed its most striking characteristic. The image has the properties of a photographic negative—that is, the light values are the exact reversal of reality. This means, of course, that a photographic negative of the Shroud image shows up as positive.

Defenders of the relic consider this fact to be proof that the Shroud image is not a mere painting. Would a medieval artist, centuries before the invention of photography, have been able to conceive of, much less produce, a negative image?

Also, the Shroud image is said to betray an uncanny anatomical exactitude. Medical investigators have claimed they could detect in the image clear signs of rigor mortis, and a sharp drawing in of the epigastric hollow (the slight depression just above the stomach) which is characteristic of a person who died while hanging by the arms.

Moreover, the body image is totally nude, and no medieval artist ever depicted Christ without at least a loincloth. In addition, the wounds are not in the palms of the hands, where medieval art always placed them, but in the wrists, which is medically and historically correct. (Nails driven through the palms could not support the weight of the body; the flesh would tear like paper.)

But if the body image on the Shroud is not a painting, how was it produced?

Several scientists—including Drs. Paul Vignon and Yves Delages of the Sorbonne, Paris, and Dr. Judica Cordiglia of Rome—claim to have demonstrated in the laboratory that ammoniac vapors emitted by a corpse enter into a stable chemical compound with spices, such as aloes, used by the Jews centuries ago in embalming. Such a chemical reaction, it is maintained, can impregnate a linen cloth with an indelible imprint of the body which the sheet wraps—and in such a case the imprint is a negative image, like the one on the Shroud.

Why assume that the image is Christ's rather than that of one of the other innumerable victims of crucifixion?

Well, the Shroud image shows a series of small punctures just below the hairline, and a large gaping wound below the heart, which matches the Gospel accounts of Jesus being crowned with thorns and having a Roman spear thrust into his side.

The Shroud of Turin is part of the unexplained, and will remain so until science is permitted to examine it directly and thus provide the answers to its many questions . . .

36. The Power of Prayer

Has prayer ever prevented an untimely death?

Consider this personal story told to me by the Reverend Eric Nash, formerly pastor of the Church of the Open Door in Hamilton, Ontario.

"About thirty years ago," he said, "during World War Two, I was doing home mission work in northern Ontario. My wife and two children were living there with me.

"The region, around a town called Massey, was then thinly populated, under-churched, and rather bleak. In winter the mercury dropped to forty below zero.

"But it never seemed so cold to me as the night I almost lost my life.

"It was near Christmas. The temperature, I remember, was twenty-nine below. I had driven in my old car to an out-of-the-way village to conduct a Bible study meeting.

"My wife Vera, not expecting me back until late, had gone to bed, planning to get up and make a pot of tea when I returned.

"However, some time after she had dozed off, my wife awakened suddenly. She was in a state of panic, and she didn't know why. A tremendous fear gripped her. And then she felt certain—though she couldn't say why—that I was in grave danger.

"A voice inside her said, 'Pray for Eric.'

"Vera knelt beside the bed and prayed that I would be spared, whatever the danger was. Her fear gradually dissolved, and a peace came into her mind. She knew, then, that the danger was past. She just knew it.

"She got up from her knees, went to the kitchen, and made some tea.

"When I finally arrived home, my wife was shocked. I staggered into the house, too weak to go any further, looking like a human icicle. I was covered with frost and half-dead from exposure.

"Vera poured several cups of hot tea into me before I thawed out enough to tell her the story.

"My old car had broken down about five miles from home. The snow was deep, and the country was deserted for miles in all directions. It was so cold it went through you like a knife.

"I had a choice—sit in the car and freeze solid waiting for help to come, or walk. I struck out on foot.

"I wasn't exactly an athlete, and the ordeal proved too much for my strength. Several times I felt all the energy draining out of me and had to sit down in the snow to get my breath. Once I thought I was really finished. No matter what happened, I couldn't take another step. This was the end.

"But as I sprawled in the snow, resigned to my fate, suddenly new strength seemed to pour into me. It was an incredible experience. I felt revitalized.

"I jumped to my feet and plunged on. By the time I reached home I was fainting from exhaustion but basically unharmed. A few days in bed and I was as good as new.

"As my wife and I discussed my close call, she told me about her feeling that I was in danger and praying for me. So far as we were able to determine, her prayers coincided with my fantastic recovery when I thought I was finished.

"How did she know my life was in jeopardy? Who told her?"

37. The Body That Didn't Decay

Can the power of the mind totally rule the body—even in death?

Paramahansa Yogananda was a yogi, or a spiritual teacher, from India who founded a society in Los Angeles called the Self-Realization Fellowship. He instructed his disciples in the ancient eastern art of mastering the body by the mind and of attaining that mystical union with God which Yoga devotees call "enlightenment."

Yogananda, as he was known to his disciples, claimed that an advanced yogi can produce phenomena which seemed incredible to most people. It was possible, he said, to put the body into virtual suspended animation, a condition so close to death that all the vital functions slowed to the point of being almost imperceptible.

Other yogis, said Yogananda, could overcome the normal processes of physical aging and decay so that, if they chose, they could live for an incredibly long time—possibly centuries.

Such exotic claims are, of course, easy to make, and the normally skeptical person will ask for evidence.

Paramahansa Yogananda offered evidence of his claims. Curiously, though, the most dramatic evidence came after his death . . .

Long before he died, the yogi predicted that he would die on March 7, 1952. On that date, Yogananda did die, apparently from a heart attack. Yet he had seemed to be in perfect health and had no history of heart disease.

Yogananda also had predicted that after his death there would be a sign that he was indeed a true yogi. The sign, so his followers believe, was that the body of Yogananda did not decay.

On his own instructions, Yogananda's body rested for 20 days after his death in a glass-topped casket. It was not embalmed or treated in any way. Yet no trace of decay occurred.

Harry T. Rowe, director of Forest Lawn Memorial Park in Glendale, California, made the following notarized statement:

"The absence of any visual signs of decay in the dead body of Paramahansa Yogananda offers the most extraordinary case in our experience. No physical disintegration was visible in his body even 20 days after death . . .

"This state of perfect preservation of a body is, so far as we know from mortuary annals, an unparalleled one . . .

"The physical appearance of Yogananda on March 27, just before the bronze cover of the casket was put into position, was the same as it had been on March 7, the day he died . . ."

When Yogananda's body was buried it exuded a strange fragrance. His followers said it was the odor of sanctity.

It has been suggested that a case such as Yogananda's could be an instance of natural mummification. But this phenomenon—in which the body tissues dry and become remarkably resistant to decay—normally is found in very hot, dry climates. If it applied in Yogananda's case, one wonders why other bodies in the mortuary hadn't exhibited the same phenomenon.

Skeptics who suggest that the body of Yogananda must have been embalmed will find it harder to explain another case which occurred long before modern methods of embalming were known.

Visitors to the chapel of the Convent of Our Lady of Mercy in Madrid can discover a casket there. In it reposes the body of a fresh-faced smiling woman dressed in a nun's habit. She looks as though she were asleep. Her face, hands, and feet, which are exposed, show no decay whatsoever.

Yet saintly Sister Mariana Navarro Romero died in 1625—nearly 350 years ago ...

38. The Haunted Shrine of Glastonbury

Is there in England a shrine which has a direct link with Jesus Christ?

The question arises from my recent visit to the ruined abbey at Glastonbury, England, where tradition says Jesus visited as a boy and where Joseph of Arimathea, the uncle of Jesus who provided the tomb for his body after the crucifixion, founded the first Christian church in Western Europe in 37 A.D.

This tradition is shrugged off by modern scholars as a pious fiction, a relic of the credulous Middle Ages. However, there are defenders of the Glastonbury tradition who argue that its claims are supported by evidence.

Well, is it possible that the young Jesus visited England and that later his uncle, Joseph of Arimathea, planted there a church—and a thorn tree?

The "holy thorn," which has grown in the grounds of Glastonbury Abbey for as long as records have been kept, is a descendant of one said to have sprung up on that spot from Joseph of Arimathea's staff. It is of a type known as the "Levantine thorn," apparently common in the Middle East, and has the charming habit of flowering at Christmas.

The Glastonbury tradition says that when he was a boy Jesus visited there with his uncle Joseph, who was a metal merchant and made frequent trips to the tin mines of Cornwall.

After Christ's death and resurrection, this same Joseph and a band of disciples traveled from the Holy Land to Glastonbury and there built a "wattle" church (one made of twigs and sticks) which was 60 feet long and 26 feet wide.

Following Joseph's death, this wattle church was encased in boards covered with lead to protect it. Later, in 546 A.D., a large stone church was built around it.

From this point, the tradition becomes firm history.

In 1184 a fire destroyed the ancient church at Glastonbury and it was rebuilt as a huge abbey housing many monks.

In 1539 Henry VIII, after his quarrel with the pope, closed the monasteries in England. It was in the next century that the Puritans burned Glastonbury Abbey. Today all that remains are magnificent ruins, which have a stark, austere beauty of their own.

Most of the "evidence" for the Glastonbury tradition is indirect and serves merely to show that the claims are at least plausible. However, a late vicar of Glastonbury, the Reverend Lionel Lewis, had such confidence in the evidence that he stated flatly: "The site of St. Mary's Church, Glastonbury, is the site of the earliest above-ground church in the world."

By comparison, he said, the first above-ground church in Rome, after the Christians graduated from the catacombs, wasn't built until around 109 A.D.—a full half-century after the traditional founding of the Glastonbury church.

Historians generally hold that Christianity wasn't introduced into Britain until the sixth century. Not so, counter defenders of the Glastonbury tradition. They cite the writings of such early church fathers as Tertullian and Origen, who lived in the second century and spoke of Britain as having already received the faith in their time.

Moreover, the tradition that the British church was founded by no less a personage than Joseph of Arimathea was no mere folk belief. It was solemnly upheld by such august church assemblies as the Councils of Pisa, Constance, and Siena, where precedence was accorded the English bishops on the grounds that Joseph of Arimathea carried the faith to Britain "immediately after the Passion of Christ."

Even English ambassadors claimed precedence on the basis of this Glastonbury tradition, as late as the time of Elizabeth I.

None of this proves anything, of course, except that the Glastonbury tradition is a venerable one, rooted in Britain's far past. But there are some further bits of evidence which make the tradition even more plausible.

Among Cornish tin miners is an ancient belief that Joseph of Arimathea was in the tin trade. That such a trade existed between England and the Middle East in the time of Jesus is well attested. Herodotus, as early as 445 B.C., speaks of the British Isles as the Tin Islands.

Further, a British archeologist, Professor Russell Forbes, had a piece of an ancient Roman drain-pipe dug up at Ostia, in Italy, analyzed, and the verdict was that the metal came from the mines of Cornwall.

Mr. Lewis, the Glastonbury vicar, claimed personal knowledge of a tradition among the villagers near the Sea of Galilee that "as a youth Jesus came to England aboard a trading vessel of Tyre."

There is another, even more curious, chapter to the Glastonbury story—a psychic one.

In 1908, extensive digging was underway for still buried remnants of the abbey. The director of excavations, Frederick Bligh Bond, was frustrated by fruitless attempts to find the site of what was known as the Edgar Chapel, after the Saxon king in whose memory it was built. Then Bond uncovered the site, in a remarkable way.

It was with a dead man's help. Or at least, so Bond said.

In a book about his uncanny experience, the archeologist told of meeting a British army officer, Captain J. Allen Bartlett, who said he was receiving communications from someone claiming to be Johannes Bryant, a monk of Glastonbury who died in 1534.

It was a map drawn by his amateur medium, said Frederick Bligh Bond, which led to the discovery of the lost chapel.

39. A Doctor Is Healed by Faith

Some doctors pooh-pooh faith healing, and James Blackann used to be one of them.

Then he was healed himself.

This Youngstown, Ohio, physician told me about his unusual experience.

It happened on a Sunday morning in May, 1968. He was attending a meeting in Youngstown's Stambaugh Auditorium, conducted by Pittsburgh-based faith healer Kathryn Kuhlman.

Dr. Blackann was there mostly out of curiosity. He had heard of extraordinary cures said to occur in the Baptist-ordained evangelist's meetings.

He wasn't there expecting or seeking to heal himself.

He did have an ailment, however—a leg condition that had been chronic for more than two years.

But he wasn't thinking of this as he listened intently to Kathryn Kuhlman. He was fascinated by the auburn-haired figure in white behind the pulpit.

Suddenly, Dr. Blackann heard Kathryn Kuhlman say: "Somebody at the back of the auditorium is receiving a leg healing at this moment."

"I was surprised to hear her say this," he told me. "The service was crowded and, as it happened, I was standing at the back of the auditorium. I looked around to see if anyone near me had responded.

Then Miss Kuhlman repeated. "This is a leg healing. Someone who's had varicose veins or some similar condition of the leg. You're not expecting a healing but you got it anyway."

"Well, this was the strangest thing to me. I had chronic phlebitis in my left leg [inflammation of a vein with resulting breakdown of tissue]. But I quickly told myself, No, that couldn't be me.

"Then Miss Kuhlman repeated, 'It's someone at the very back of this auditorium.'

"And again I thought, That couldn't be me. Why, I haven't even asked for help!

"Instantly I heard Miss Kuhlman say, 'No, you haven't asked for help but you've been healed anyway. Take it and let me know.'

"Then she went on with the service."

Later, on his way home, Dr. Blackann realized, with genuine disbelief at first, that the condition he had suffered for months had gone. His leg seemed perfectly normal.

"And I had a bad case of phlebitis," he said. "The car door had slammed on my leg two years before. I had severe pain and swelling—lots of it.

"The extreme medical procedure is to go in surgically and

debride—that is, cut out—the affected tissues and muscle. That leaves a hole in the leg which eventually heals.

"Well, I was in hospital for a while. I didn't have the surgery because we were able to get the blood supply back to the affected area. However, it left very severe pain. That went instantly when I was healed."

How did Kathryn Kuhlman detect that somebody at the back of that crowded auditorium had a leg condition, related to the veins, which was being healed?

Dr. Blackann said that even in the unlikely event that the evangelist had spotted and recognized him in the meeting, he hadn't mentioned his ailment to her and no one else could have.

"You see," he explained, "only my wife and I knew about my leg."

The curious phenomenon of instant diagnosis of disease, and a knowledge of where and when they are being healed in the congregation, is a regular feature of Kathryn Kuhlman's ministry.

She can't explain this phenomenon—a sort of medical clairvoyance or ESP—any more than she can explain the healings themselves.

"You can't analyze the way the healing power works," the evangelist once told me, "any more than you can analyze God. It's God who performs these healings. I'm just a bystander."

Since his own experience, Dr. James Blackann says he has witnessed other, more extraordinary things in Kathryn Kuhlman's meetings.

"I've seen massive cysts disperse," he said. "I've watched spastic conditions disappear. I've witnessed arthritic spines instantly freed."

How?

As a doctor, James Blackann can't answer that.

But simply as a human being, he murmurs: "God has no limits."

40. Healing by Words

It is an extraordinary fact that words can heal. Yes, words alone.

Consider the phenomenon of hypnosis being used to treat a variety of diseases. In the hypnotic state, the subject's conscious mind is temporarily anesthetized so that suggestions can be fed directly into his deep mind. And these suggestions—which, of course, consist of *words*—can produce startling physical results.

A New Jersey physician, Dr. Howard B. Miller, reported to the American Society of Clinical Hypnosis in November, 1969, that he had regressed six cases of inoperable tumors by hpynotherapy. He reported success in treating blood and skin disorders, too.

One of the most extraordinary cases of healing through words was reported in the *British Medical Journal* of August, 1952. It concerned a disease named icthyosis which was treated hypnotically by a London physician, Dr. Albert Abraham Mason.

Icthyosis—literally, fish-scale disease—is an ailment, usually congenital, in which the suffer's skin hardens into a black, rough casing that sometimes covers most of the body.

The patient treated by Dr. Mason was a 16-year-old boy whose whole body was affected except the chest, neck, and face. The boy had been born with the disease, and attempts to treat him by grafting normal skin from his chest to the affected parts proved useless. The grafts rapidly turned black and scaley like the rest of his skin.

Dr. Mason decided to try hypnosis after everything else had failed.

In a hospital in East Grinstead, Sussex, he put the boy into a trance while a dozen skeptical doctors watched. The procedure took 10 minutes. Then Mason said again and again, in a low, even voice: "Your left arm will clear."

The idea of starting on a particular part of the body was to focus the suggestion.

About five days later the coarse layer on the boy's left arm became soft and crumbly and flaked off. The skin underneath was pink and soft. In 10 days the whole arm was clear.

Gradually, in response the repeated hypnotic suggestions, the parts of the boy's body affected by the icthyosis became 90 percent clear.

Dramatic as it was, the change in this case could not properly be called a cure. If the hypnotic suggestions were not repeated weekly, the disease symptoms started to return. To prevent this, the boy learned self-hypnosis and was able to maintain the improvement by this means.

Since an organic disease was involved here, and not one rooted in emotional causes, the influence of the hypnotic suggestions was particularly significant. It is one thing for hypnosis to benefit an ulcer, or some other stress-induced illness, but quite another for it to clear up a disease which was present from birth.

Words express ideas and beliefs, of course, and in this case the healing was produced by a change in the subject's believing—a change brought about by hypnotic suggestion.

PART IV

Mysteries of ESP

41. The Man Who Blasted Clouds Out of the Sky

Can "mind power" blast clouds out of the sky?

A man named Rolf Alexander claimed that he could disintegrate clouds by willpower at a distance of 10 miles. And, bizarre as this claim sounds, it was supported by some provocative evidence, including photographs.

Alexander gave numerous public demonstrations of his purported cloud-blasting ability. One took place on September 12, 1954, in Orillia, Ontario, where he was then living.

In the presence of more than 50 witnesses, including the mayor of the town and a contigent of reporters, Rolf Alexander asked a bystander to select a group of fluffy cumulus clouds, and then pinpoint a single cloud in this group as "the target." The adjacent clouds served as "controls." (If the demonstration was valid, only the target cloud should be affected.)

Alexander narrowed his eyes, breathed deeply and evenly, and a curious thing occurred. The target cloud enlarged slightly, then quickly shrank until nothing was left. The whole process of disintegration, which was photographed at intervals, took eight minutes. The control clouds remained virtually intact.

Coincidence?

Well, the experiment was repeated three times that day with different groups of clouds. Each time the results were the same—the target cloud, chosen by someone other than Rolf Alexander, disintegrated, while adjacent clouds remained substantially unchanged.

Alexander (who died a few years ago in Miami) claimed that he dissolved the clouds by a force projected from his mind.

"Anyone in good health can be taught to do it," he used to say. "I don't claim to have any special occult or mystical powers."

Alexander said that the same power could be used to heal, or to influence the behavior of other people.

"The reason I use clouds," he explained, "is that there can be no collusion between me and a cloud."

There is some negative evidence to consider in assessing the phenomenon of cloud-blasting.

Though Rolf Alexander's claims stand or fall by the evidence and not by his personal character, it is a matter of record that he served two jail terms—one in Florida in the 1920's for mail fraud, the other in California in the 1940's for practicing medicine without a license.

Meteorologists pooh-pooh Alexander's claims. Their argument is that fair weather cumulus clouds such as he used in his demonstrations generally disappear in 15 to 20 minutes, anyway.

But this argument ignores the fact that Alexander used control clouds. If his demonstrations were based on sheer coincidence, why did only the target cloud disintegrate? In Britain, a crew from Independent Television filmed eleven demonstrations by Alexander, and in every one the target cloud, and only the target, vanished within 10 minutes. The film was telecast on the program "This Week."

Moreover, on several occasions Alexander, on demand, varied his performance. Instead of making the cloud disappear he would, if asked, burn a hole through the middle of it, like a doughnut.

Perhaps one way to settle the argument about cloud-blasting is to try it yourself. Rolf Alexander suggested that with practice most people could do it. And he left fairly explicit directions.

"Look at the target cloud," he instructed, "then shut your eyes quickly and mentally photograph the cloud. Get a vivid image of it in your mind. Then, with your eyes still shut, visualize what you want to happen to that cloud. See it disintegrating, step by step, until it's gone.

"Then open your eyes. Stare at the cloud and breathe rhythmically—counting to five on the inhalations and to eight on the exhalations. Concentrate on the idea that power is going out from you, through your eyes, to that cloud. Will it out of existence."

42. The Power of Negative Thinking

A curious experiment has yielded startling evidence that the power of positive thinking may be no match for the power of negative thinking.

The experiment was designed to test whether human thought can directly influence plant growth.

Considerable research already had been done in this field. The Reverend Franklin Loehr, a Presbyterian minister-chemist, wrote a book titled *The Power of Prayer on Plants,* (published by New American Library as a Signet paperback) which reported that prayer made a significant difference in plant growth when all other conditions were standardized.

This was corroborated by Dr. Bernard Grad, a biologist at Montreal's McGill University, who did a series of prayer-on-plant experiments using a self-styled faith healer named Oskar Estebany. The prayed-over plants in Grad's experiments grew significantly better than the control ones which did not receive prayer.

However, when Dr. Grad asked neurotic and psychotic persons to pray for plants, they produced an apparent inhibition of growth.

Grad's conclusion: Positive thought can stimulate cell growth, whereas negative thought seems to retard it.

This is where I came in.

Using as guinea-pigs the members of my adult education class in parapsychology at Toronto's Ryerson Polytechnical Institute, I set out to measure, if possible, the relative effects of positive and negative thinking. Or, as we decided to call it, "blessing" and "blighting," respectively.

The experiment was to test the following hypothesis: "If identical seeds receive standardized treatment, and in addition one group is blessed while the other is blighted, the first will grow significantly better than a control group, and the second significantly less."

My first problem was how to divide the class into the three groups consisting of controls, blessers, and blighters.

Then I had a hunch.

Early researchers in parapsychology found that when they tested subjects in ESP card-guessing experiments, most of them, as expected, scored only at the chance level. A few scored significantly above chance. These were called "psi-hitters" (psi here being a general term for psychic ability, or ESP).

However, there was a third group called "psi-missers." These were people who made significantly *fewer* correct guesses than they should have by chance alone. Their scores were often as dramatic as those of the psi-hitters—but in reverse.

Researchers came to believe that these statistically significant misses were deliberate on the part of the unconscious mind. In a sense, they represented disguised hits, or negative hits.

The hunch was that psi-hitters would make good positive thinkers, or blessers, for the experiment; and that psi-missers would make good blighters.

So the class was divided according to their scores on an ESP card-guessing test: those who guessed correctly at the chance level became the control group; those above the chance level were the blessers; and those below the blighters.

For the experiment—which was to last 14 days—we used barley seeds from the same bag that were planted in identical soil in identical peat pots.

Seeds in the control group received only sunlight and water. Those in the blessed group received, in addition, 15 minutes a day of positive thoughts. The blighted seeds received the same period of negative thoughts.

After two weeks, the seedlings were measured, root and shoot, by a biologist who, according to the "blind method," wasn't told anything about the nature of the experiment.

These measurements were then given to a mathematician who, similarly ignorant of the experiment, was asked to make a statistical evaluation.

The difference between the control seeds and the blessed seeds was not significant (although, as a matter of fact, the blessed seeds did grow slightly better than the controls).

However, the difference between the blessed seeds and the blighted ones was striking.

The blighted seedlings averaged less than half the growth of the blessed ones—6.0 centimeters compared to 12.7.

More startling was the fact that 62 percent of the blighted seeds did not even germinate—although the puzzled biologist could find no trace of disease on them. By contrast, not a single one of the blessed seeds failed to germinate.

The mathematician calculated that the odds against such differences being due to chance were 1,000 to 1.

What is also significant is that E. Douglas Dean, formerly president of the Parapsychological Association, tried the same experiment and duplicated the results.

Can negative thinking, like some death ray, freeze the life out of barley seeds?

If so, what else could it possibly blight?

43. Strange Literary "Coincidences"

Literature bristles with curious coincidences which suggest that the writer saw more clearly perhaps than even he knew.

One of the most astonishing scientific lucky guesses—if that's what it was—appears in *Gulliver's Travels*, where the author, Jonathan Swift, mentions that Mars has two satellites.

The fact, of course, is that Mars does have two moons— but they were not discovered until 1877. Or, 151 years after Swift mentioned them.

The book, published in 1726, was actually titled *Travels Into Several Remote Nations of the World by Lemuel Gulliver,* and the relevant passage is as follows:

"Certain astrologers have likewise discovered two lesser stars, or satellites, which revolve around Mars, whereof the innermost is distant from the center of the primary planet exactly three of its diameters, and the outermost five; the former revolves in the space of ten hours and the latter in twenty-one and a half . . ."

Swift's description of the two moons corresponds closely to reality (which is even more startling than his mentioning the fact of their existence). One satellite travels around Mars in 7 hours and 39 minutes, and the other in 30 hours 18 minutes.

Their distance from Mars is approximately what Swift said.

As a matter of fact, one of the moons, Phobos, goes around Mars in the same direction as the planet rotates but in only one-third the time, so that it appears to rise in the west and set in the east. This is the only known body in the cosmos which revolves around a central planet faster than that planet itself rotates. And all this is indicated in Swift's description.

It was a century after Swift's book was published before a telescope was even invented powerful enough to see the moons of Mars.

How, then, did Swift write about them, and with such accuracy, when no astronomer on earth knew they existed?

Another striking example of the literary imagination projecting itself forward in time is found in the works of an eighteenth-century Serbian named Roger Boscovitch.

A Jesuit priest and a scientist, Boscovitch wrote about things which belonged 200 years in the future. For example, he considered in detail such modern ideas as:

• The creation of an international geophysical year for the pooling of scientific data (which finally came about in 1957-58).

• The transmission of malaria by mosquitoes (a fact not proven until the early twentieth century).

• The existence of other solar systems besides our own.

Like Einstein, two centuries later, Boscovitch proposed a unitary theory of the cosmos which would embrace physics, chemistry, biology, and all other physical phenomena.

Again, the same question: How did the writer describe discoveries not made for 10 generations?

44. Out-of-the-Body in the Laboratory

Some people claim to have had the experience of temporarily leaving their bodies.

Vivid imagination? Fantasy?

No doubt many such experiences are. In the uncanny phenomenon known as "autoscopy," the person sees a projection of his own body image. This sort of experience is not pathological nor even abnormal; people as distinguished as

Sigmund Freud and Ernest Mach, the Austrian physicist, had autoscopic hallucinations.

However, is there a type of out-of-the-body experience which goes beyond autoscopy? In other words, can some people really leave their bodies?

Dr. Charles Tart of the psychology department of the University of California at Davis has done pioneering laboratory research into out-of-the-body experiences. His prize subject was a young women who said she had had such experiences since childhood. In a report on his research, Dr. Tart calls this woman, a college student, Miss Z.

During one of her typical out-of-the-body experiences, Miss Z would awaken from sleep, she said, to find herself apparently floating near the ceiling. She could see her physical body lying on the bed below, yet she—another part of herself—was outside that body. This other part was the thinking, feeling part of her.

In his experiments with Miss Z, designed to sift possible fact from fantasy in her experiences, Dr. Tart divided the laboratory into a sleeping room for her and an observation room for himself, with a large viewing window between.

In the sleeping room was a cot and scientific equipment to measure the subject's brain-wave activity, heart rate, respiration, and circulation.

About six feet above the cot—and this is significant—was a shelf bearing a clock and a small card on which numbers could be written.

For the experiments, Miss Z was hooked up to the machines which monitored her physiological functioning. She couldn't move more than two feet from the cot without tearing loose the wires, therefore it wasn't possible for her to see either the clock or the small card on that shelf six feet above her. On the card Dr. Tart had written a random five-digit number.

The task assigned to Miss Z was to read that number.

The experiment continued four consecutive nights. On the second night Miss Z reported getting partway out of her body, as she put it, so that she caught a glimpse of the clock but couldn't read the number on the card. The time, she said, was 3:15 A.M. And she was right—that was indeed the time when she reported herself partway out of her body.

On the fourth night, at 6:40 A.M., while Dr. Tart was monitoring his instruments, Miss Z reported leaving her body completely, floating up to the ceiling, and reading the number on the card. She said it was 25132—and she was correct.

Interestingly, while she was reporting this experience, her brain wave patterns were different from those of persons who are sleeping, awake, or in a coma. Nor did she have the rapid eye movements (REM) which accompany dreaming.

45. Voices From Nowhere

The air around us, we know, swarms with sounds and images accessible only by means of radio or television receivers. But are there other sounds or images we don't normally perceive?

The experiments of a Latvian engineer named Konstantin Raudive suggest that we are surrounded by mysterious sounds which lie beyond the threshold of normal hearing. Raudive, by means which he professes not to understand, appears to be able to pick up, on an ordinary tape recorder, inexplicable voices.

They are, if you like, voices from nowhere.

A British electronics engineer named Kenneth Atwood was recently invited to an experimental session with Raudive at the home of London publisher Colin Smythe. Atwood took with him a highly tuned tape recorder from a well-known British company and several sealed blank tapes.

These new tapes were played while the instrument was turned to recording and everybody in the room remained silent.

"In the playback," said Atwood, "voices came through on the tapes. They were low and seemed to be speaking in foreign languages."

It's reported that the bodiless voices have spoken in Russian, Latvian, German, Spanish, and English. Some of the communications appear to be personal ones directed to people present at the session. Others are of a general nature and purport to come from such notables as John F. Kennedy, Winston Churchill, Leon Trotsky, and even Adolf Hitler. (Hitler is said to have blamed his worst crimes on the fact that he had syphilis of the brain, and to have begged for-giveness.)

Konstantin Raudive, whose integrity is vouched for by a number of prominent scientists, says he has been picking up the mysterious voices for six years. He believes they are communications from the dead. He claims that he himself often hears from his deceased mother.

Other experts who have studied the "Raudive phenomenon," as it's come to be called, don't know what to make of it.

The electronics engineer, Kenneth Atwood, said, "I don't think they're freak radio transmissions, but they're definitely voices. I don't doubt Mr. Raudive's integrity either."

In other words, the tapes, in Atwood's opinion, were not faked.

A Swedish psychologist, Irma Millere, who has studied the mystery of the voices for several years says she is stumped.

"Maybe," she suggested, "it will take the work of several generations to unravel the complicated riddle."

What do the voices say? Here the mystery deepens. One would expect the dead, if they do speak, to say something significant. But many of the utterances Raudive has recorded consist of remarks like: "Churchill here ..." "Everything goes well with us ..." "Is the weather nice there?" and similar trivialities.

Some researchers have suggested that Raudive's unconscious mind may release a psychic force which imprints the voices on the audiotape.

The phenomenon remains *unexplained*.

46. Today's Fiction— Tomorrow's Fact

History written in advance? It can't be, of course. And yet ...

Consider the story of Morgan Robertson and one of his novels. Robertson, a noted writer of sea stories, penned the saga of a huge, opulent Atlantic liner, loaded with rich and complacent people, which during an April voyage hit an iceberg and sank with virtually everybody on board. The name of Mr. Robertson's fictional ship was the *Titan,* and she had been declared unsinkable.

Besides the name of the ship and the circumstances under which she sank, there were other obvious parallels between the fictional vessel and the famous ship, the *Titanic,* which of course sank in the Atlantic in April after hitting an iceberg. Both ships, the *Titanic* and the fictional *Titan,* had too few lifeboats; the *Titan* had 3,000 persons aboard and 24 lifeboats, the *Titanic* 2,207 persons and 20 lifeboats.

Both ships had a top speed of 25 knots. In the novel, the vessel's displacement was 70,000 tons, while the *Titanic*'s was 66,000 tons. The fictional liner's length was 800 feet, that of the *Titanic* 882 feet. Both ships had three propellers.

It would be comforting if Morgan Robertson's novel, *Futility,* published by M. F. Mansfield, New York, was clearly a fictional rewrite of the true story of the *Titanic,* and not a too imaginative one at that. The only trouble with this theory is that the novel was published in 1898—fourteen years *before* the wreck of the *Titanic* and several years before the construction of that glittering ship was even contemplated.

Instead of the familiar fiction based on fact, which we're all used to, what we have here looks suspiciously like fact based on fiction.

There are even stranger cases of fact following fiction.

In 1856 and 1870, the French author Jules Verne wrote two novels about man's first voyage to the moon. He might have been writing about the actual first manned moon landing by Apollo XI in 1969, a century later.

There were three astronauts in Verne's fictional spacecraft, and there were also three Apollo XI astronauts. In both fiction and fact, the launching site was in Florida. Verne named his Cape Town and gave it a location close to the present Cape Kennedy. The fictional spacecraft was named the *Columbiad*; the Apollo XI command module was the *Columbia.*

The French novelist said that his craft, traveling at about 25,000 miles an hour, would reach the moon in just over four days—or, to be exact, 97 hours and 13 minutes. The Apollo XI craft, traveling more than 24,000 miles per hour, reached the moon in approximately 97 hours and 30 minutes.

Verne's fictional spacecraft even splashed down in the Pacific—a hundred years before the real thing happened.

Another eerily prescient bit of science turned up in a book called *The Manual of Spherical Astrology*, published in Paris by Vigot Brothers in 1897. On page 316 of that book appeared the statement:

> "A planet exists beyond Neptune.
> It will be called Pluto."

Thirty-four years later, in 1931, the American amateur astronomer Clyde Tombaugh discovered a planet beyond Neptune which did come to be called Pluto.

But fact not only follows written fiction, it follows films too.

Alfred Hitchcock's movie *The Birds*, based on a short story by Daphne du Maurier, was about flocks of normally harmless birds attacking and killing human beings. In May, 1960, after the movie was released, a group of schoolchildren in Leicester, England, were dive-bombed by screaming magpies, just as in the film. The victims received deep gashes in their heads, hands, and ears before the birds were driven off.

Since magpies are inoffensive creatures, the attack was mystifying. But not unique. In January, 1969, Derek Reegan awoke to find his house in Peterborough, England, beseiged by thousands of starlings, which normally flee from man. The birds flew in from the dark, beating their wings furiously against windows and assaulting doors with their beaks.

I wonder which of today's fiction will become tomorrow's fact?

47. The Shadow Returns

Remember The Shadow?

He was the mysterious nemesis of crime who held millions of readers and radio listeners spellbound in the 1940's.

By day he was Lamont Cranston, "wealthy man about town," whose faithful companion, "the lovely Margo Lane," was the only person to know The Shadow's true identity.

By night he swooped on evildoers, a black-cloaked crusader whose chilling laugh struck terror into his enemies.

"Who knows what evil lurks in the hearts of men?" went the famous line. "The Shadow knows." And then came the icy, spine-tingling laugh.

Well, recently I met The Shadow. Or at least the next best thing to it. I met his creator, Walter B. Gibson, alias Maxwell Grant, under which pen name he wrote no less than 385 full-length novels about The Shadow. Gibson, an irrepressible talker brimming with energy and still churning out books (80 at last count), is a fascinating, many-sided personality.

An amateur magician, he knew intimately most of the great stage illusionists of the 1920's and 1930's—Thurston, Blackstone, Dante, and the most famous of them all, Houdini. Gibson ghost-wrote one of Houdini's books.

His wife, the beautiful Litzka, is the widow of another celebrated illusionist, The Great Raymond, and a magician in her own right. She and Gibson for many years had a pet rooster named China Boy who was house-trained and, according to Gibson, was "more psychic than most people."

Yes, Walter Gibson believes in the psychic. Though he's been around magicians most of his life and knows all the tricks, he's convinced there is such a thing as a genuinely inexplicable phenomenon. And he's had numerous such experiences.

"Once, while writing The Shadow novels," said Gibson, "I spent several weeks at a pleasant old inn outside of Philadelphia.

"Late one night, I finished a final chapter ahead of schedule, so I decided to take the story to New York the next day. I left the manuscript on the table in perfect order, then I opened the window, turned out the light and went to sleep.

"Hours later, I was awakened by a flapping of the window shade. A wintry breeze was blowing, but I was too tired to get up and close the window, so when the flapping lessened, I went back to sleep. Later, I had this dream:

"I was in the editor's office in New York. I gave him the manuscript and he began reading the first few pages, as he often did. Suddenly, he asked, 'Where's page four?'

"I started looking through the manuscript and found that page four was missing, so I pawed wildly through the remaining pages in search of it. With that, I woke up.

"It was just dawn and time to get up. Naturally, I was glad that experience had only been a dream, but as I closed the window I looked toward the table and saw that the breeze had blown a few dozen pages from the manuscript so that they were lying face down near the table edge.

"Several pages had drifted to the floor but they were still overlapping and therefore in order, so I replaced them on the stack.

"During breakfast I described the dream in detail and when I went back to the room I was still chuckling 'Where's page four?' as I put the manuscript in my briefcase, intending to give it a final check during the train trip to New York.

"That was when it struck me that I ought to make sure that page four was really there.

"It wasn't. Hastily, I pawed through the pages as in my dreams. Still no page four. I looked under the table, in the wastebasket, under the bed, but no luck, until I decided that it had to be under the bed because it couldn't possibly be anywhere else.

"So I took a flashlight and actually crawled beneath the wide double bed to make a final probe. There, clear back against the wall, blown practically upward by some wayward gust, was the missing page four."

Gibson cites this as an example of a "clairvoyant" dream—that is, one in which ESP operated. The purpose, in this case, was obvious. To prevent his leaving that hotel room without the missing page four.

A dramatic example of a premonition is cited by Gibson's wife, Litzka. It happened when she was married to Maurice Raymond, who circled the globe seven times as "The Great Raymond," master of magic.

While touring South America, the Raymonds were booked for an important engagement in a city that could only be reached by a two-day trip on a river steamer. On the day of scheduled departure, after the Raymonds' 20 tons of equipment had been loaded and the 25 persons in their party had already gathered at the dock, Litzka announced that she wouldn't go anywhere on that boat.

Why? Well, she had a "feeling," that's all.

Accordingly, the equipment was unloaded and put aboard another, smaller steamer which made the trip safely and uneventfully.

Later, the Raymonds discovered that the first boat had run aground and taken on water. If it had been carrying their equipment, that, no doubt, would have been ruined and the boat might well have sunk.

Gibson calls this "a pure case of precognition in which you simply know that something must be avoided though there is no apparent reason why."

Of course, The Shadow might know why . . .

48. Veiled Pictures of What Is to Be

In a 1968 book titled *Prophecies of World Events by Nostradamus*, U.S. writer Stewart Robb predicted that in 1973 a Middle East War would break out between Israel and the Arab states and prove to be the first act in an apocalyptic 27-year conflict, leading to the biblical Battle of Armageddon.

Well, the Yom Kippur War flared in October, 1973. But the rest remains unfulfilled . . . yet.

It's not surprising in this age of turmoil and anxiety that end-of-the-world doomsters are flourishing, or that they cite Nostradamus. This French astrologer and seer, dead more than 400 years, is the most renowned prognosticator of all times—credited with feats that put every other prophet in the shade.

Nostradamus is credited not only with fixing the dates of events that occurred long years, even centuries after his death—the great fire of London, for example, and the proclamation of the French Republic—but also with giving the names of the people not yet born when he wrote.

He is said to have described the rise and fall of Bonaparte, the convulsion of the French revolution—including the execution of the king and queen—and Drake's defeat of the Spanish Armada. Among modern events, this sixteenth-century prophet is credited with foreseeing air warfare and the submarine, the collapse of the Maginot Line and France's partition by the occupying Germans, the Nazi blockade of Britain, and the overthrow of Hitler, whom he is said to have mentioned by name.

The skeptics retort that Nostradamus wrote in puzzles, and each reader finds in the cryptic prophecies exactly what he wants to find. Apparent hits, say the skeptics, are sheer coincidence.

Here's a look at history's most celebrated prophet and a few of his most notable predictions—some allegedly fulfilled, some yet to be.

Nostradamus is the Latin form of the name of Michel Notredame, who was born at St. Remy, France, on December 14, 1503. He took a medical degree, then attracted considerable fame by his skill at casting horoscopes, eventually becoming court astrologer to King Henry II and his Queen, Catherine de Medici.

In 1558, Nostradamus published the first edition of his soon-to-be-famous *Oracles*—354 rhymed quatrains containing veiled pictures of what was to be.

In the foreword he described how the oracles came to him while he sat with a magic wand staring into a fire. Apparently some sort of angelic being appeared to him and imparted the prophecies. He died in 1566.

Interpreting Nostradamus' prophecies before the event is exceedingly difficult, if not impossible, since they are replete with coded meanings, symbols, and word plays. It's said that the prophet had to be prudent about making his meaning too clear lest he anger someone in authority.

An example is a prophecy of Nostradamus' that his admirers claim was fulfilled during his lifetime. It is said to have predicted the death of King Henry II. Here are Nostradamus' words:

> The young lion shall overcome the old on
> the field of war in single combat;
> He will pierce his eyes in a cage of gold.
> This is the first of two loppings, then he
> dies a cruel death.

Witnesses said that Nostradamus applied this particular oracle to the King and had spoken of it to Henry himself.

In 1559, the French king, wearing his emblem, the lion, and a gold helmet, challenged a young nobleman named Montgomery to a friendly joust. Montgomery, whose emblem was also a lion, accidentally pierced the king in the eye through the visor of his gilt helmet. After lingering in great pain for several days, the king died.

Nostradamus' supporters then decided the symbols: The "old lion" was the king; the "cage of gold" in which his eyes were pierced was the gilt helmet he wore, the "first of two loppings" was later seen as referring to the untimely death of the king's son, Henry III, who fell by the hand of an assassin.

Since Nostradamus was French, and close to the royal family, it would not be surprising if related themes figured prominently in his oracles. One such prophecy proved to contain an obscure proper name.

The oracle spoke of somebody called "the Great Montmorency" who, through rebellion against "the Dauphin," would be delivered to "famous punishment." These last two words are in French *"clere peyne."*

On October 30, 1632, the second Duke of Montmorency, who styled himself "the Great," was beheaded for treason against the king, Louis XIII, who had been, as it happened, the first man since Nostradamus' death to bear the title "Dauphin" (or, consecrated heir to the throne of France).

The most striking thing, however, is that Montmorency's executioner was a common soldier, chosen by lot, whose name was Clerepeyne.

This is either one dilly of a coincidence or something else. Could someone have written this prophecy after the event and attributed it to Nostradamus?

A British researcher, Rupert Gould, subjected the prophecy and fulfillment to exacting scrutiny. He concluded that, incredible as it seems, the oracle linking Montmorency to "clere peyne" was indisputably in print some 75 years before the event.

Critics are driven to distraction by Nostradamus' habit of hiding names in word plays and anagrams. The reader finds himself wondering whether claimed correspondences between a particular prophecy and event really exist or are merely some quirk of the mind which starts seeing what it's told to see. Or is it all some odd series of coincidences?

In several quatrains which seem to pertain to the French revolution, Nostradamus, writing 200 years before the events, cites proper names. In one, he speaks of the king being betrayed by "Narbon and Saulce."

Now it happens that Louis XVI's minister of war was dismissed for suspicion of being in conspiracy with the republicans. His name was Count Narbon, the mayor of the town of Varennes, where Louis and his queen, Marie Antoinette, were arrested while trying to flee the country, was singled out for special praise by the republicans for having apprehended the royal couple. The mayor's name: Saulce.

In another dated prophecy, Nostradamus spoke of a "great persecution of the Christian Church to culminate in the year

1792 which people will think to be the renovation of the age."

This is said to have been fulfilled with the closing of all churches in France by the republicans and the proclamation of Year One of the Republic which began on September 21, 1792.

Nostradamus foretold the coming of an emperor of the French who would be born near Italy, rule for 14 years, then end his days on "a chalky island in the sea." Napoleon was born on Corsica, which is near Italy, was in supreme control of France from 1799 until his abdication in 1814, and died in exile on St. Helena, a rockpile in the Atlantic.

It's claimed that Nostradamus used an anagram for Napoleon's name when he wrote of *"Pau.nay.loron."* (the periods are in the original). Take out the letters "roy," instruct the Nostradamus buffs (because this means "king) and you're left with Pau.na.lon. Reverse it and you have Na.pau.lon.

What the ordinarily skeptical person is likely to ask is, Why, if the prophet could foresee Napoleon's name, didn't he simply write it correctly? Wouldn't that have been infinitely more convincing? And how could it possibly have endangered him more than a century after his death? Or was it that the prophet sometimes saw through a glass darkly?

Coming to modern times, Nostradamus is credited with anticipating the horrors of modern warfare:

> Living fire and death hidden in
> globes will be loosed, horrible,
> terrible.
> By night, enemy forces will reduce
> cities to powder.

But is this more than poetic imagination of a sort shown by other writers who claimed no special prophetic powers?

More intriguing are three quatrains in which Nostradamus refers to "Hister," which has been taken to be an anagram of Hitler.

At first reading, the most important of these seem particularly lucid:

> Liberty will not be recovered.
> A bold, black, base-born, iniquitous
> man will occupy it;
> When the material of the bridge is completed
> The republic of Venice will be annoyed by Hister.

Some Nostradamus buffs, combing through obscure news stories of World War Two, have identified the "bridge" in his oracle as one the Nazis built over the Danube at Sofia in 1941. The "republic of Venice" being "annoyed" is supposed to refer to the beginnings of the falling-out between Nazi Germany and Facist Italy (although what the bridge had to do with that isn't clear).

"Hister" is said to be "Hitler" with the "l" replaced by an "s" and its position slightly changed. Skeptics contend that Hitler is an ancient term for the Danube River and obviously refers to that.

What of Nostradamus' visions for our future?

A quatrain often cited as describing the end of the world says:

> The year 1999, seventh month,
> A great king of terror will descend
> from the skies ...

This has been taken to refer, variously, to a cataclysmic battle between the human forces of good and evil; an intervention by God Himself; or the arrival on earth of a spaceship.

Whether it means any of these, or anything at all, is for you to decide.

49. Suddenly, Inexplicably, the Nail Bent

Can Uri Geller really zap metal with his mind?

It's said of the 27-year-old former Israeli paratrooper that he bends spoons with his eyes, that forks curl up when he looks at them, stopped watches start like magic when he passes his hand over them, and under his gaze gold rings melt on their owner's fingers.

Geller, who now lives in New York, is the hottest exponent of the art of psychokinesis, or PK—the claimed ability of some people to influence physical objects directly by the mind. Call it mind over matter.

Today, a growing number of scientists are willing to take a serious look at PK and similar phenomena once dismissed out of hand as supersitition or cheap tricks. Even the Pentagon is rumored to have sat up and taken notice of Uri Geller's strange doings. There's talk in some quarters of an "Esp race" between the U.S. and Russia, and a new word has appeared: ESPionage.

Already Geller has been a guinea pig at California's prestigious Stanford Research Institute, a think-tank that does classified work for the U.S. military. Two SRI staffers, Dr. Harold Puthoff and Russell Targ, experts in laser physics, said that Uri performed feats under "cheat-proof" conditions "that science cannot explain."

Among other things, Geller is reported to have moved a balance inside a vacuum jar; guessed correctly 12 times in a row which one of the 10 identical metal cans contained an object; and predicted eight times out of eight which number would show up on a die shaken in a box. (The odds against this were a trillion to one.)

Accusations of fraud have been made against Uri Geller since he did a stage and nightclub act six or seven years ago in Israel. He denies heatedly that his PK performances were ever "exposed" as trickery, and a spokesman for the Israeli consulate in New York denied published reports that Geller left his native land in 'disgrace'."

On the question of trickery, consider a personal experience of mine with Geller that, for all my background in psychical research and in detecting fraud, I found genuinely puzzling and convincing.

Geller said that he would try telepathically to pick up my thoughts. He asked me to make a simple drawing of anything, which he would attempt to reproduce.

I went to a nearby room and, after posting a lookout at the door, took a piece of my own paper, and, using the wall as a writing surface, drew a simple picture of a tree. Placing it in a opaque envelope, and sealing the envelope, I put the drawing in my inside coat pocket. Then I rejoined Geller and several others.

Geller asked me to concentrate on my drawing and "I'll try to see it on this television screen I have inside my head." We were sitting four feet apart. Geller did not touch the envelope containing the drawing, which I held between my palms.

"I see something that looks like—I don't know what it looks

like," he said. "It's sort of a mushroom cloud, the kind you see after an atomic explosion."

He sketched something quickly and held it up.

It was, as he'd said, like a mushroom cloud, and it was also an almost exact replica of my tree.

To top off the demonstration, Uri said he would try to zap some metal with his mind. While I held a one-inch steel nail I had brought with me between my thumb and forefinger, Geller gently stroked it.

Suddenly, inexplicably, the nail bent.

Were those tricks?

Well, being not unwise in the ways of magic I was on guard against possible fraud.

There are several methods by which mentalists gain access to secret drawings (for example, by having the person make the drawing on a trick clipboard with a hidden carbon that provides a copy of everything written) but I did not detect Geller's employing any of them.

Bending the nail? Well, a magician would do this—or appear to do it—by making a fast switch, substituting an already bent nail for the straight one. But I had deliberately kept firm hold of the nail at all times.

What Geller did on that occasion continues to impress me. However, on another occasion he performed two off-the-cuff feats that were not convincing at all.

We were having lunch and Geller was talking about his mysterious powers (as he usually does) when suddenly he lifted his menu and, behold, his fork was grotesquely bent. His powers had done it, he announced. However, I couldn't help noting that Geller, who is a very strong young man, is left-handed and his left hand was concealed under the menu when the fork was bent.

Later, while the two of us were in an elevator, he was telling me how objects sometimes "teleported" into his presence, when suddenly something clattered to the floor. It was a knife from the dining room where we had just eaten. The knife had been "sent" to show his powers, Geller said, but a less exotic theory that occured to me is that it could have been up his sleeve.

If an individual were gifted with genuine ESP and PK, would he, or could he, ever cheat?

This conundrum has bedeviled modern psychical research since it began more than a century ago. Time and again, psychics who on one occasion appeared to have shown absolutely genuine phenomena, on another occasion were caught in trickery. Human nature is complex, and who can know it?

Besides demonstrating PK, Uri Geller is now making very unusual claims that even some of his avid supporters find hard to accept. He says that he is in communication with super-intelligent computers from outer space, possibly another galaxy, who are preparing him for a great mission.

These messianic claims have emerged since Geller was befriended two years ago by a New York physician, parapsychologist, and drug researcher, Dr. Andrija Puharich. Geller himself told me that until he was hypnotized by Dr. Puharich he knew nothing about the extraterrestrial computers and their mission for him.

Puharich tells amazing stories. He says he has seen Geller board a flying saucer that he, Puharich, was prevented from boarding. He says that he has watched while Geller "dematerialized" and "rematerialized" physical objects. On one occasion, says Puharich, Geller teleported a camera 6,000 miles from Puharich's home in Ossining, New York, to Tel Aviv.

Uri himself, and his business manager Yasha Katz, told me that they split all the money Geller makes with Puharich (including, presumably, the $50,000 advance Puharich recently got from Doubleday for a book about Geller). Geller and Katz were matter-of-fact as they recounted for me some of Geller's latest marvels. Once, they said, he teleported a television set into a hotel room.

"The damn thing came right through the ceiling," Geller said, looking me straight in the eye.

After a moment's somewhat strained silence, Yasha Katz added "It was a color set, too . . ."

50. Fate's Scenario

Shakespeare said that all the worlds a stage and our lives are like actors' roles. But does that mean that what happens to us is scripted in advance?

If so, one man got a peek at the scenario and found that it included murder.

William Terriss was a British actor who on the night of

Thursday December 16, 1897, was to appear in a mediocre melodrama called *Secret Service* at London's Adelphi Theatre. The actor's understudy in the part was one Frederick Lane.

On the afternoon before the performance, Lane came to rehearsal. He was very upset and described a vivid and ominous dream he had had the night before. He insisted on buttonholing everybody in sight to tell them about the dream.

Lane said he had dreamed that William Terriss, surrounded by actors and stagehands, was lying unconscious on the stairs leading to the theater's dressing rooms. His chest was bare and blood was streaming from a gaping wound.

Lane insisted that the dream had been peculiarly realistic. But his listeners pooh-poohed him and no doubt suggested that he stop eating spicy foods before going to bed.

That night, December 16, the unthinkable happened.

As William Terriss entered the Adelphi Theater to prepare for his performance, he was savagely attacked and stabbed by a madman. Carried inside, the dying actor was laid at the foot of the stairs leading to the theater dressing rooms—exactly as his understudy, Lane, had dreamed it the night before.

True to the best show-must-go-on tradition, *Secret Service* was performed that night with Frederick Lane in the starring role.

We know that these events happened. Three members of the cast signed affidavits that Lane had told them of his dream the afternoon before Terriss was slain. The names of the witnesses were Frances Hygate, Carter Bligh, and Creagh Henry.

A last spooky touch is lent to this story by an unusual sequel which was recounted to me by writer Walter Gibson, creator of the famed mystery character The Shadow.

Gibson told me how, in the early 1950's, he was writing and narrating a radio series on the unexplained. One of the stories he researched was this case of the uncanny death of William Terriss.

The day he finished writing the script, while the story was very fresh in his mind, Gibson and his wife went to a garden party. One of the first people Gibson met was a stranger who said his name was Terriss.

"Funny thing," said Gibson, "I've just finished writing about the strange death of an English actor named Terriss."

"Yes," replied the stranger, who had an English accent, "he was my grandfather."

51. Call for Help

On Wednesday, May 25, 1960, tidal wave warnings sounded across the Hawaiian Islands.

Mrs. Emmet G. North was home alone when the alarm came. Her home was in the threatened area. But Mrs. North was unable to seek safety because she was confined to a wheelchair.

Her husband was out of town on business. Mrs. North tried to get help by phone, but the storm had blown down the lines. She was trapped while somewhere out there the tidal wave was rolling relentlessly toward her.

In her plight, the woman tried to send a mental call for help. She attempted to reach someone, anyone, who could help her.

"I'm trapped, I need help," she sent out her thoughts.

Meanwhile a visitor from Idaho, 70-year-old Thomas Powers, drove past the North home. He was looking for the house of friends who lived in the neighborhood, but he had lost his way. He had no idea there was a tidal wave alert, in spite of the radio reports, because he was deaf.

But something led Thomas Powers to stop his car a half-block past the North home. He sat for a moment with the motor idling, then slowly backed up. He stopped in front of the North home. Something seemed to be prodding him to go into that house.

He laughed at himself and was about to drive away when the feeling grew stronger. Powers shut off his motor and got out of the car.

Feeling slightly sheepish, he walked to the door of the house and knocked.

Immediately, Mrs. North called for help from within. Powers, of course, couldn't hear her. But something prodded him to try the door, to open it, and go into the house.

He found Mrs. North, obviously in a state of panic. In spite of his deafness he grasped immediately the peril they were both in. He assisted the women to his car and drove away.

Fifteen minutes later the tidal wave pounded in and swamped that neighborhood.

Where did the impulse that prodded Thomas Powers into acting as he did come from?

Was it mere coincidence?

Or ESP?

52. Journey into the Past

Can you walk through time into the future—or the past?

Most of us are accustomed to thinking of time as a river that flows irresistibly in one direction only. But does that river ever turn back upon itself?

On August 10, 1910, two highly esteemed Englishwomen experienced a foray into what some might call a time-warp.

Charlotte Moberly was principal of St. Hugh's College, Oxford, and her companion, Eleanour Jourdain, served as her secretary. The pair were sightseeing in Versaille, France.

Like many other tourists, they visited the Petit Trianon, one of the sumptuous palaces built by Louis XIV in the seventeenth century, and later lived in by the ill-fated Louis XVI and Marie Antoinette, who lost their heads during the French Revolution.

As they entered the garden of the Petit Trianon, both Englishwomen sensed a strange, unsettling atmosphere. Somehow, nothing about the place seemed right. They met people—a gardener, soldiers, a woman in splendid clothes—who looked mysterious and ethereal.

The Englishwomen heard these people speaking French but being excellent linguists, they recognized it as an unfamiliar, archaic-sounding French.

They came across landmarks of which they could find no trace on their detailed maps. Odd, uncharted paths appeared.

A pretty woman dressed in a long-outmoded cape sketched in a garden but didn't look up as they passed. However, a man with a pock-marked face whom both women later described as "evil-looking," seemed to be following them.

In the distance, a band played unfamiliar music, although no band could be seen anywhere.

Curiously, no other tourists appeared during the time the two Englishwomen were in the garden. When they emerged from it, they felt as though some heavy cloak had been lifted from their shoulders—a cloak of dread.

Miss Moberly and Miss Jourdain, both brilliant scholars, checked all the historical records meticulously. They discovered that the garden they had visited was identical to what it had been in 1798—a hundred years before their time.

The French they had heard spoken was the language of that bygone era. The clothes worn by the people they had seen were the fashions of a century before.

Later, when the women returned to the garden it bore no resemblance to the one they had visited earlier. Everything was different—paths, landmarks, and especially the atmosphere, the feeling about the place. Gone was the dread.

The two women called the account they wrote of their experience, "An Adventure"—as indeed it had been. An adventure into the past ...

53. The Premonitions Bureau

Are you a human seismograph that can pick up the foreshocks of a disaster before it strikes?

If so, science wants you.

It all started back in 1966 when, early on the morning of Friday October 21, an elderly man in northwest England had a peculiar dream.

He saw, spelled out in dazzling letters, the word ABERFAN.

The word meant nothing to him—until he heard a radio news report later that day.

A gigantic slag heap had thundered down a mountainside into a Welsh mining village, engulfing a schoolhouse and burying 128 children and 16 adults.

The name of the village: Aberfan.

Then it came to light that all across Britain, for two weeks before the disaster, human seismographs had been quivering from the foreshocks of the disaster. Careful checking of many of the claimed premonitions was done by London psychiatrist Dr. J.C. Barker and he found sixty that were exceedingly well documented.

In Aberfan, the morning of the tragedy, a 9-year-old girl named Eryl Mai Jones told her mother: "Mummy, I dreamed last night that I went to school and there was no school there. Something black had come down all over it."

At 9:30 that morning Eryl Mai was one of the children in Pantglas Junior School buried under a half-million tons of coal waste.

Dr. Barker, the investigating psychiatrist, noted that some of the premonitions were more or less literal forecasts of the disaster, while others were in symbols, albeit symbols easy enough to interpret after the event.

One woman, for example, dreamed two days before the coal-slide of "hundreds of black horses thundering down a hillside dragging hearses."

In a dream the night before the tragedy another woman saw a procession of children dressed in the Welsh national costume ascending to Heaven.

Dr. Barker wondered, Can this strange ability that some people have to sense a coming calamity be put to practical use?

In January, 1967, he formed the British Premonitions Bureau. People were invited to send in their dreams or impressions which they felt were precognitive. Hopefully, these would not only add to scientific knowledge but form the basis of an early warning system of disaster.

In its first year of operation, the premonitions bureau received 500 predictions of natural disasters, plane crashes, political upheavals, deaths of notables, assassinations, etc.

By the end of the year, six persons had emerged as particularly reliable seismographs. Unusually accurate predictions about the Robert Kennedy assassination, for example, came from these people.

In 1968 the former Central Premonitions Registry was established in New York by *New York Times* staffer Robert D. Nelson and his wife. It has received a steady stream of dreams, hunches, visions, and just plain guesses—more than 2,000 to date. Some have been strikingly accurate.

Late in the summer of 1970, a housewife in Bridgeport, Connecticut, wrote to the registry that "President Nasser of Egypt will suffer a sudden attack—chest region or upper torso—by the end of the year." On September 28, two weeks later, Nasser dropped dead from a heart attack.

One prediction received by the registry in December, 1968, looks positively eerie in the light of political events in Washington.

A young Englishman, Malcolm Bessent, as part of a series of long-range predictions, wrote: "Starting with 1972-73 it will be a crucial year for the U.S.

"Water everywhere, resulting in social upheaval, anarchy and political confusion. The people will be looking for a new leader."

"Water everywhere?"

A symbol of Watergate?

54. The Dream That Changed History

Dr. Robert Van de Castle is one of the world's leading dreamologists. In an interview, this psychology professor at the University of Virginia School of Medicine talked with me about the largely unsuspected impact dreams have had on the world.

In the arts, for example, dreams have yielded a rich harvest.

The composer Tartini dreamed that the Devil was playing a wild piece of music on the violin: written down upon awakening it became, appropriately, *The Devil's Sonata.* Coleridge said his poem *Kublai Khan* came to him intact in a dream. And Robert Louis Stevenson received the plots of many of his stories, notably *Dr. Jekyll and Mr. Hyde,* in dreams.

Scientific breakthroughs, too, have been inspired by dreams.

The great physicist Niels Bohr dreamed of being on a sun composed of exploding gasses while planets attached by thin filaments whirled around it; from this came his epoch-making model of the atom with electrons orbiting the central proton.

However, one dream which had a devastating influence on modern history, and the fate of millions, had nothing to do with art or science.

It occurred in 1917, during the First World War, to an obscure soldier, a corporal, who was sleeping in a front-line trench in France. The dream, disturbingly real, was of a tremendous explosion followed by a dense shower of mud and molten metal. The corporal's chest was covered with blood. He felt himself smothering. His cries for help were strangled in his throat.

The dreamer awakened—shaking, gasping for breath, sweat streaming down his face. Restless, he climbed out of the trench and strolled in some nearby fields. Though he realized he was in imminent danger from enemy fire, he felt safer than in the trench.

Suddenly there was a thunderous blast nearby, and the corporal flung himself to the ground. When the dust cleared, he saw that the trench he had just left had received a direct hit from an enemy shell. A huge mass of earth had rained down upon the trench, and several of his comrades were buried—as he had been in his dream.

That dream catastrophically changed the course of modern history because the corporal was Adolf Hitler.

55. Hitler: The Black Magician

After the Berlin premiere of the movie *Hitler: The Last 10 Days,* a middle-aged German housewife said, "It didn't catch his black magic."

This image of Hitler had been conjured up before. In 1937, a dinner companion of the Nazi Führer said: "When he stares at you with those burning eyes you know you are in the presence of a madman—a madman who is also a black magician."

Now a book has appeared which claims that Hitler was indeed a black magician—in the literal, not the figurative sense. Written by former British Commando Officer, Trevor Ravenscroft, it alleges that Hitler's power for world domination came from a sacred relic—the "spear of destiny" that pierced Christ's side when he hung on the cross—which was turned into an evil talisman.

The author's exotic theory is that Hitler saw the spear in a Vienna museum where it was kept on exhibit and intuitively realized its power as an instrument of sorcery. When he took over Austria, says Ravenscroft, Hitler seized the spear and used it in black magic rituals.

The book is utterly crazy, of course. But the image of Hitler as a black magician, as someone, that is, whose sources of power defy wholly rational explanation, is a different matter. The modern world's most evil genius eludes neat, conventional categories.

Many shrewd observers marveled at the uncanny way he had of seeing through people and situations.

"The Führer," intoned German industrialist Wilhelm Keppler to an English friend in 1933, "has direct telepathic contact with higher powers."

While planning his assault on Russia he assured his assembled generals "I feel the spirit of prophecy stirring in me once again."

Delusions of grandeur? Probably. Certainly at the end Hitler showed clear symptoms of outright madness. But was there something else lurking behind the madness?

His early feats as a military strategist were incredible. Whether Hitler himself took the advice of atsrologers is a moot point (though many top Nazis did), but by coincidence or not, his brilliantly successful *blitzkrieg* attack on Holland was launched at precisely the time, May 10, 1940, even to the hour, that an astrologer would have recommended.

Consider, too, Hitler's uncanny knack for escaping death. At least 17 known death traps were set for him during the 1939-45 period. He escaped them by his eerie intuition and uncanny luck.

Historians attest that the day before the celebrated bomb attempt on his life on July 20, 1944, Hitler told his luncheon companions: "I know they're going to try to kill me very soon. I feel it."

When the dictator staggered out of the wrecked building in which four men lay dead, though he was virtually unhurt, he was shrieking: "Who dares to say now that I am not under the special protection of higher powers!"

Previous "miracles" had contributed to the mystique of Hitler's charmed life.

In March, 1943, General Henning von Tresckow, in a conspiracy with other Wehrmacht officers, placed a bomb aboard a plane in which Hitler was returning from an inspection of the Russian front. The bomb was set to explode in 30 minutes. It didn't.

Later von Tresckow retrieved the unexploded bomb, examined it, and found that the mechanism had worked perfectly. The fact that the bomb had failed to go off he called "an inexplicable thing."

A still earlier attempt to kill Hitler misfired. On November 8, 1939, he suddenly left a Munich beer hall ahead of schedule, and minutes later a bomb in the speaker's rostrum went off, killing seven people on the platform.

On another occasion, a Wehrmacht colonel with a live bomb in his pocket tried to get close enough to Hitler to blow both himself and the Führer to bits. But Hitler raised his head, like a wild animal sniffing the breeze for enemies, and abruptly left the room.

During World War II many German homes had a "Führer shrine" complete with candles and a picture of Hitler. Stories appeared in the German press about how Allied bombs had wrecked a house but left the wall bearing Hitler's picture still standing. And in 1944, Nazi cabinet minister Robert Ley actually called for Hitler to be "raised to our altars" as a god.

Yes, however you interpret the words, Hitler was a black magician.

56. The Devil's Astrologer

Wilhelm Wulff was the devil's astrologer.

This Hamburg star-gazer served during World War II as a member of the court of Heinrich Himmler, Hitler's infamous chief of the Gestapo and the S.S.

Against his will, Wulff says—it was a case of cooperate or be sent back to the concentration camp where he had spent several months—he cast daily horoscopes for the most hated man in Europe. His predictions evidently were accurate enough to keep his job and his freedom.

Herr Wulff, with whom I talked recently and found to be very articulate at 82, offers some insights into the macabre affinity between Naziism and the murky world of the occult.

Hitler, of course, had a mystical faith in his own destiny ("I go the way that Fate has appointed," he once said, "with the confidence of a sleepwalker") and he set great store by his dreams. It's fortunate that he did, since it was one of

Hitler's dreams that held up the production of Germany's V-1 and V-2 rockets until it was too late for them to decisively influence the outcome of the war.

In 1941, "The Führer had a dream that the rockets will never reach London," said an aide, and work on the project was virtually suspended for two years.

Rudolph Hess, Hitler's beetle-browed deputy-führer who startled the world by flying to Scotland in 1941 on a self-styled peace mission, was cracked on anything occult. Palmistry, crystal balls, faith healing, strange diets—he believed them all.

There is evidence that Hess was influenced in his flight by his staff of astrologers who convinced him that he had a "great mission" to bring peace between Germany and her Anglo-Saxon cousins.

Wilhelm Wulff first was conscripted to work for the Nazis at an Institute for Occult Warfare in Berlin. There, under government sponsorship, various occult practitioners, from trance mediums to pendulum-swingers, were paid to come up with something, anything, which would help Germany win the war.

"I felt as though I were in a madhouse," says Wulff, who, although an astrologer, is capable of skepticism.

In 1943 he came to the attention of Himmler, who was very interested in the occult, and was assigned to work under Arthur Nebe, head of the Gestapo's criminal branch. Wulff was given birthdates of persons unknown to him and asked to rate them as "security risks." He did well, apparently, well enough so that soon he was invited to join Himmler's entourage.

Then started a bizarre nightmare. Wulff had to prepare regular horoscopes indicating what Himmler should and shouldn't do, which dangers he should watch for, whether plots were brewing against him, and so on.

He quotes Himmler as saying to him at one point: "It's strange, isn't it, that you warned me about a possible accident on December 9 and on that date I was driving at night, and 130 feet above the Black Forest railway I ran off the road and onto the track just as the train was approaching.

"The accuracy of your horoscopes, Herr Wulff, is phenomenal."

Possibly the most important task Wulff was given was to find the missing Mussolini. That was in 1943, just after the Duce had been overthrown by a palace revolt and disappeared. Hitler suspected he had been kidnapped and ordered his rescue at any cost.

Wulff says that he cast the sort of horoscope for finding somebody's whereabouts—he doesn't describe how one does this—and came up with the conclusion: "Mussolini is somewhere to the southeast of Rome, not more than 75 miles from the city."

This was, in fact, the case. At the time, Mussolini was imprisoned on the island of Ponza off the Italian coast, within the area specified by Wulff. (However, he was soon moved to a mountain fortress from which Hitler's paratroopers eventually freed him.)

Wulff describes the last time he saw Himmler, on April 24, 1945. The most feared man in Europe was himself trembling with fear because of the impending Allied victory.

The tyrant, as Wulff pictures him, had become a whining, cringing blob of jelly.

Thus ended Himmler, and Wulff's curious, hazardous, and still ambiguous career as the devil's astrologer.

57. The Psychic S.O.S.

When we're in trouble, do we transmit?

To put it more plainly, when people are in a crisis situation, can they broadcast a psychic S.O.S.—a call for help?

The late great medium Arthur Ford, whose biography I've written (*Arthur Ford: The Man Who Talked with the Dead*, published by New American Library as a Signet paperback), had several such experiences.

One time, Bill Wilson, the famous founder of Alcoholics Anonymous and a good friend of Ford's, was walking down a New York street when he felt a powerful urge to go to the medium's apartment. Wilson, intent on important business, fought the impulse but it grew stronger.

"I was practically forced to go to Arthur's apartment," he said later.

He found the door open, the phone off the hook, and Ford unconscious on the floor, gasping with a heart seizure. Wilson called the doctor and Ford's life was saved.

On another occasion, in Chicago, on May 10, 1966, Arthur Ford was chatting with a friend, Arthur Shefte, in his suite at the Palmer House Hotel when he suddenly pitched forward and sprawled unconscious on the floor.

Forty miles away, in her home in Park Forest, Illinois, Marguerite Harmon Bro, a clergyman's widow and a noted editor and writer, was awakened from an afternoon nap with the sudden impression, "Get in touch with Arthur Ford quickly. He's in danger."

Mrs. Bro, a close friend of Ford, knew that he was staying in Chicago and immediately called his hotel room. She was told by Shefte that Ford had collapsed just a moment before—there hadn't even been time to summon a doctor.

There was trouble getting a doctor, but through Mrs. Bro's frantic phone calls Ford was rushed to Chicago's Weslet Memorial Hospital where his friend Kenath Hartman was the administrator.

Ford was found to have a blood pressure in the upper two hundreds and an embolism in the lung. He probably would have died if he had gone more than 20 minutes without an oxygen tent.

The most dramatic such incident involving Arthur Ford occurred in January, 1968. Ford, unknown to anybody, was lying critically ill in his Philadelphia apartment, victim of a massive heart attack.

At the same time Dr. Edwin Boyle, a Miami cardiologist, was attending a medical convention in New York.

Dr. Boyle told me he had a sudden urge to look up Arthur Ford. He had never met the medium, though he had read about him, and he tried to dismiss the feeling as a curious whim.

"Why, I didn't even know where Ford lived," Boyle said, "though I seemed to recall a medical colleague once mentioning that it was Philadelphia."

The cardiologist checked the Philadelphia directory and found Ford's address. He tried to phone him but there was no answer.

By this time, the curious whim had turned into an inexplicable compulsion. It was as though an inner voice was chorusing, "Go to Arthur Ford. He needs you."

Dr. Boyle took the train to Philadelphia and proceeded to the Westbury Hotel where Ford lived. When his knocks at the door brought no answer, he summoned the desk clerk and got a key to Ford's room.

The two men found the elderly medium stretched out on the floor in a coma. Dr. Boyle administered emergency treatment and Ford revived.

But the mediums first words to his medical rescuer were, "Who the hell are you?"

But the most curious part of this curious story comes now. For after Boyle had arranged for an ambulance to take Ford to the hospital, the phone in the apartment rang. The doctor answered it, identifying himself.

The call was from a prominent United States senator, a friend of Ford's. He was phoning from Washington because, he said, "My daughter has been bugging me all day to call.

"Last night she had a vivid dream in which Arthur Ford was in grave danger and needed our help."

This amazing story was told to me both by Dr. Boyle and the senator whose daughter had the strange dream.

58. Warnings—From Where?

During World War II, Winston Churchill, Britain's prime minister, was getting into his car when, as he put it, "Something said to me, 'Stop.' "

Churchill stopped.

Turning away from the door, which as usual was being held open for him, he got in the other side of the car where he sat during the journey.

Shortly after, a German bomb landed nearby. The blast tossed the car up on two wheels, and but for Churchill's extra weight on the raised side it would have turned over.

Later, remarking on the incident, Churchill said that after he heard the "something" telling him to stop, he had felt directed to get in the other side of the car and stay there.

This case is one of many similar experiences collected by Dr. Ian Stevenson of the University of Virginia. A number of them occurred, like Churchill's, in Britain during the heavy bombing of World War II.

Does the stress of wartime bring to the surface human faculties which normally lie dormant?

In such experiences, the warning may not be for the person

who receives the impression but for someone else. And it is not always possible to prevent the impending misfortune.

At the beginning of May in 1941, Mrs. Rosalind Heywood, a writer, stood chatting on a London street with Dr. Gilbert Murray, the celebrated classical scholar.

Pointing to the Houses of Parliament nearby, Murray remarked, "Well they haven't hit them yet."

At these words, Mrs. Heywood almost cried aloud, Oh, don't say that!

The sudden impression knifed into her that the Parliament buildings would be hit by a bomb the following Saturday. She felt perfectly certain of it.

She also had the impression that her husband's club, which was nowhere near the Parliament buildings, would be bombed the same night.

As it happened, that night both the Parliament buildings and her husband's club received their only direct hits of the war.

Moreover, because of Mrs. Heywood's warning, her husband, who had to stay at his club that night, left his room to take shelter—the only night during the war he did so—and saved his life. His room was demolished in the bombing.

In another case, during an air raid on an English town, a young girl begged her parents not to take refuge in the family bomb shelter in the garden.

"Something," the girl said later, "told me not to go."

Her parents hesitated. The next moment a bomb hit the shelter, obliterating it and most of the garden.

These experiences prompt many questions for which at present we are short of answers.

For example, in such cases where does the mysterious warning originate? In the person's own unconscious mind? Does his own ESP sense the impending danger?

If so, why don't such warnings come more often?

59. The Strange Hymn

It was a Sunday and the Reverend Charles Morgan, minister of Rosedale Methodist Church in Winnipeg, Canada, arrived at his church to prepare for the evening service.

The custom was for the choirmaster to choose the hymns and Mr. Morgan to post them on the hymn board. He did this, then went to his study.

There was considerable time until the service and he dozed off.

The minister had a strange dream. He saw only a surging darkness but distinctly heard in the dream an old hymn—one he used rarely, if ever, in church. In fact, he hadn't sung the hymn in years. But now his dream was filled with it, accompanied by a sound like rushing waters.

The minister awakened, oddly disturbed, the hymn still ringing in his mind. He glanced at his watch. There was plenty of time until the service. He dozed again.

Once more he dreamed of the same hymn, now sung by a chorus of voices. And still, in the background, the sound of surging, crashing waters—*angry* waters.

Mr. Morgan awoke with a start. His dream weighed heavily on him. Why, he didn't know.

He got up from his chair and walked out into the still-empty sanctuary. As though in some sort of mystic thrall, only half aware of what he was doing, he looked up the hymn from his dream and posted the number on the hymn board.

Later, in the service, it was the first hymn the congregation sang. It seemed a little out-of-place in a church thousands of miles inland—"Hear Father, while we pray to Thee, For those in peril on the sea . . ."

During the singing, the minister was surprised and embarrassed to find his eyes filling with tears.

The date was April 14, 1912.

Only later did the Reverend Charles Morgan discover that at the very time his congregation was singing that hymn, one of history's greatest sea tragedies was unfolding in the North Atlantic.

The *Titanic* was sinking.

60. The Husband in the Deep Freeze

Between husband and wife, ESP isn't all that uncommon. But rarely is it, as it was for Dennis and Mary O'Brien, a matter of life and death.

Dennis O'Brien worked as manager of an ice cream factory in Manchester, England. His house was some two and a half miles from the factory.

One Saturday night in December, 1959, Mary O'Brien, expecting her husband to be late getting home, settled down to watch television. But she couldn't relax. Though her husband was often late, and she normally was unconcerned, this was different.

"I felt what I can only describe as butterflies in my tummy", Mrs. O'Brien said, "rather as you feel before a dentist's appointment.

"I had never worried about my husband before. I always just went to bed and slept. But this night it was impossible for me to sit and concentrate on anything."

Mrs. O'Brien phoned the ice cream factory but there was no answer. Later she tried twice more with the same result. She assumed that her husband was away from the phone; possibly he already had left for home.

But he did not arrive, and Mary O'Brien's inexplicable anxiety grew stronger. Finally she decided to do something she never had done in the several years her husband had worked at the ice cream factory.

"I took the risk of leaving my two-month-old daughter in her bed alone—something I would never have done under normal circumstances and have never done since," said Mrs. O'Brien. She hurried to her husband's factory.

She found the door to the factory locked. By this time Mary O'Brien felt sheer panic. She took it upon herself to break a window and climb in—fortunately for her husband.

"I found him huddled in what he called the cold store—the walk-in refrigerator," she said. "He had been careless and accidentally locked himself in.

"On comparing notes we discovered that it had happened only minutes before I felt the urge to phone the factory for the first time.

"Needless to say," added Mrs. O'Brien, "had I not had this premonition, or whatever it was, my husband might have frozen to death."

Dennis O'Brien confirmed his wife's story. He too noted that it was quite unlike her to feel concerned about him at work.

"It's absolutely true," he said, "that my wife had never before, to my knowledge, shown any signs of distress or worry however late I got home from the job—even a late as six A.M."

And never, since the incident, had Mrs. O'Brien felt a similar concern.

It is not uncommon for wives to worry about their husbands. But the skeptic who wishes to dismiss this case must explain why, out of all the times Dennis O'Brien had been late, his wife chose the night he was in actual danger to experience her strange premonition.

Coincidence? Or something more?

61. The Persistent Mother-in-Law

On the night of Wednesday August 3, 1966, Mrs. Brigitte Judd of Upland, California, had an overpowering feeling that her mother-in-law was trying to get in touch with her.

The feeling was unusual for at least two reasons: first, Mrs. Judd and her husband had not been on speaking terms with his parents since a family squabble two years before; and second, her mother-in-law lived in the same town and could pick up the phone if she wanted to communicate.

Yet, absurd as it seemed, Mrs. Judd's feeling grew into a compulsion. And then she had a startling "vision"—a sort of waking dream—in which her mother-in-law and father-in-law appeared to her.

"I actually saw my mother-in-law," said Mrs. Judd, "and my father-in-law with her. They were standing in front of our master bathroom with their hands extended toward me.

"The appearance or picture was so real that I stretched out my hand. But before I touched them I told myself this is nonsense, they're not here, you're just overtired. With that, the figures vanished."

Mrs. Judd's husband, noticing her stunned expression, asked what was wrong and she told him. Without a word he jumped in his car and drove to his parents' home. It was in darkness and nobody was there.

A few days later, on Saturday, Mr. Judd showed his wife a story in the newspaper about his parents. They were reported overdue on their return from a fishing trip to Mexico. The

Judd's knew nothing of any such trip. Brigitte Judd wondered if it could have anything to do with her strange experience.

Five days later, the missing parents were rescued after drifting for 12 days in the Gulf of California. The engine of their small cabin cruiser had failed and the craft was swept far away from the coastline and help. When finally rescued, the couple were near death from dehydration.

This ordeal healed the family rift. Brigitte Judd's mother-in-law said that during the days they were drifting she thought of Brigitte and her husband a great deal and the fact of being alienated from them weighed on her conscience.

Significantly, Brigitte Judd said she had first had the feeling that her mother-in-law was trying to contact her a week before her strange vision. This was exactly the time when her mother-in-law's ordeal on the drifting boat began.

Was Mrs. Judd's feeling and vision prompted telepathically by her mother-in-law's thoughts about her?

If feelings and thoughts can reach through space, from one mind to another, the universe is more mysterious than many people think.

62. A Famous Writer Sees the Future

Occasionally experiences occur which raise the question: Is the future like a blueprint, already mapped out?

If not, how could novelist Taylor Caldwell have been told exactly when and how her writing career would skyrocket from dismal failure to dazzling success?

In January, 1938, Taylor Caldwell and her husband chanced upon a spiritualist meeting in Buffalo, where they were living. Both of them were depressed, since the novelist had just received word that a thousand-page manuscript which a New York publisher had previously agreed to put out as a book had, in fact, been rejected.

So, discouraged and sick at heart, the novelist and her husband found themselves at a psychic demonstration in Buffalo's Statler Hotel conducted by a medium from England named Charles Nicholson.

"I get a message from an Arthur," the medium murmured. "Is there anyone here whose father is named Arthur?"

"That was my father's name," Taylor Caldwell offered cautiously.

"Your father," the medium promptly replied, "is trying to tell you not to be discouraged. He knows you have just had a bitter disappointment but he wants you to know that the manuscript will be published and be a great success.

"The manuscript, he says, will be sold on April 2 of this year to another publisher. It will establish you as a writer.

"And in addition," continued the medium, "a year from now, after the book has been published, you will be in Hollywood working on a motion picture version of the book."

The message sounded impossible to Taylor Caldwell and her husband. Yet there was no way the medium could have known she was a novelist who had just had a manuscript rejected. Or was there?

At any rate, the predictions were too outlandish to be true.

However, on April 2, 1938, Taylor Caldwell signed a contract with another company for the publication of her manuscript. The book, titled *The Dynasty of Death,* became an overnight best-seller and established her as a major literary figure.

And oh yes . . . a year later the novelist and her husband were in Hollywood, where she was writing the screenplay based on her novel.

This is the amazing story Taylor Caldwell tells . . .

63. Pain Through Space

Can a person experience pain being suffered by someone else, five thousand miles away?

Here is a case, investigated and documented by Dr. Ian Stevenson of the University of Virginia, which suggests as much.

On October 17, 1959, Mrs. Dora Martin awoke in Naples, where she and her husband were vacationing, with some alarming symptoms.

"I had severe pain in my chest and a terrible feeling of depression," Mrs. Martin recalled. "It was as if someone had put a black cloak over my shoulders. I started to cry. I told my husband that I hadn't cried in nine years but the tears were running down my face.

"Physically, I felt like the air was slipping away from me. I felt like someone was taking the air out of my lungs so that I couldn't breathe."

Mrs. Martin's husband, a physician, examined her but could find nothing wrong to account for the symptoms.

"My wife," he recollected, "had not been ill for months before this episode, nor was she ill for months after. Furthermore, the episode was unusual in that it not only involved discomfort but also a feeling of depression and anxiety which was foreign to her normal cheerful outlook."

Mrs. Martin stayed in bed for three or four hours, then the mysterious symptoms passed as suddenly and unaccountably as they had come. She got up and, in her words, "felt fine the rest of the day."

It was Mrs. Martin's husband who suggested that her peculiar attack might have something to do with her twin sister, Mrs. Martha Morrison, who, back home in Philadelphia, was pregnant. The baby wasn't due for three months, but the Martins wondered if complications had developed.

Their intuition, they later discovered, was accurate.

On October 17, in a Philadelphia hospital, Martha Morrison gave birth, three months prematurely, to a baby girl. The delivery was extremely difficult and Mrs. Morrison was left exhausted.

Then, later in the day, she developed blood clots throughout her body, localizing in her lungs.

"I woke up with an inability to get my breath," she recalled. "My chest felt like one cramp after another, stabbing in the front and coming out the back."

Mrs. Morrison's account of her symptoms was corroborated by her obstetrician.

Taking into account the difference of five hours in local time between Philadelphia and Naples, it appears that Dora Martin awakened with her baffling symptoms when her twin, Martha, was suffering her attack of blood clots in the lungs, half a world away.

Psychiatrists are aware that people can pick up another's symptoms through intense emotional identification with that person. Thus, a middle-aged woman complained of severe pain in her right shoulder for which medical examinations could discover no cause. Eventually, it was learned that short-ly before her illness began, the woman's son had died of cancer of the gall bladder and the pain had been "referred" through the nervous system to his right shoulder.

What is different in the case of the twin sisters, Dora and Martha, is that they were separated by thousands of miles and there was no normal communication between them. However, evidence suggests that there was communication of some sort so that the one sister felt in her own mind and body the distress which the other was experiencing.

64. A Psychiatrist's Psychic Experience

When a person reports that he's had an ESP experience, one of his friends is sure to advise him, jocularly or other-wise, to see a pyschiatrist.

But what if the one who has the experience is a psychia-trist?

Dr. Jerrold Hammond, a child psychiatrist formerly at the University of Virginia medical school, recounts a dramatic experience while he was serving as an American army officer in World War II.

The time was January, 1945. The incident involved a Ger-man V-1 rocket, hundreds of which, at the time, were raining down on London where Hammond was stationed.

"The rockets made a rather loud noise until the motor cut out just before the bomb dropped," Dr. Hammond recalled.

"After a little experience, it became possible to judge ac-curately how far away the bombs were. If you considered a bomb near, there was usually time to take shelter. If the bomb seemed distant, you didn't bother to take shelter."

"At the time of the incident, Hammond had six month's ex-perience in judging how near a particular flying bomb was. None had landed close enough to put him in any danger.

But one night, while he was staying in a London hotel, he heared the peculiar put-put sound of a flying bomb. He judged it to be quite distant—at least three miles from his ho-tel. That meant he was in no danger.

As he continued to listen to the rocket engine, however, he suddenly was seized by an urgent impulse to take cover.

"The feeling seemed quite irrational," Dr. Hammond had anticipated.

The blast blew in the windows of his room and sprayed the bed with chunks of debris and razor-sharp shards of glass. Anyone in the bed would have been perforated by the jagged, spear-like glass fragments.

Was the impulse to take cover a mere coincidence? A lucky guess?

Against this theory Dr. Hammond cites the fact that "this was the only occasion on which I ever had a strong impulse to take shelter.

"And this was the only occasion when a bomb fell as close to me as this one did."

65. The Strange Journey of Henry Stanley

Henry Stanley, the man who said, "Dr. Livingstone, I presume," once took a journey stranger than his famous search for the celebrated missionary doctor in the jungles of Africa.

During his twenties, Stanley (later Sir Henry) was living in the American South. When the war between the states erupted, he joined the Confederate army. Captured by Union forces at the Battle of Shiloh in April, 1862, he was sent to Camp Douglas in Illinois.

On the morning of Wednesday April 16, 1862, Henry Stanley was playing cards with some other Confederate prisoners of war. Suddenly he felt a soft touch on the back of his neck and lost consciousness.

He regained consciousness immediately, it seemed to Stanley, to see clearly the village in Wales where he had been born and raised. He later wrote that he seemed to be floating above the familiar grass-covered hills. Then he glided into the house of his aunt Mary and into her bedroom, where he found her dying.

Stanley discovered himself beside his aunt's bed, listening to her last words. She seemed to be trying to tell him she was sorry she hadn't been kinder to him when he was a child. He heard himself saying that he, too, as a child, had been unable to express the real affection he felt for her.

They clasped hands, and the aunt breathed a farewell.

The next instant Henry Stanley awoke with a start. He was back in the prisoner of war camp, the other Confederate soldiers with whom he was playing cards staring at him intently.

"What happened?" Stanley stammered, trying to collect his wits.

"What do you mean, 'What happened?'" one of the prisoners replied quizzically. "What could have happened? Only a moment ago you spoke to me."

The experience, which to Henry Stanley had seemed to take a considerable time—half an hour at least—had actually transpired in a moment.

Was it a vivid waking dream? A strange hallucination?

Well, Stanley later received word that his aunt Mary, back home in the mountains of Wales, had died on April 17, 1862. This was within a few hours of the time at which he had the eerie experience of being at her deathbed.

66. Mind Reading or Messages From the Dead?

In September, 1967, I presided over the first attempt to call up the dead on prime-time television.

That was the celebrated seance in which the late Bishop James Pike said he believed he had spoken with his dead son through the famous medium Arthur Ford.

In my biography of Ford (*Arthur Ford: The Man Who Talked with the Dead*), I revealed that evidence discovered in the medium's private papers indicated that he cheated in the Pike seance.

Ford, it seems, went to the seance crammed with research on Bishop Pike. He had a passion for clipping obituaries, and much, though not all, of his most evidential messages could have come straight from that source.

One newspaper clipping, the obituary of the Right Reverend Karl Morgan Block, Pike's predecessor as Bishop of California, contained all the personal details which Pike found convincing when Block purportedly communicated.

However, though Arthur Ford apparently fell back on trickery at times—possibly when his alcoholism weakened his powers—he gave evidence of being a genuinely gifted psychic.

Consider this extraordinary case.

In 1929, Arthur Ford gave a public demonstration of "clairvoyance" in Boston's Jordan Hall. He picked out of the audience of several hundred a man he had never met— Joseph Carlton Beal, a member of the editorial staff of the *Boston Transcript*.

Beal was utterly skeptical of alleged psychic powers— Ford's or anybody else's. He was the author of a satirical novel, *Romances of Matilda*, which contained a blistering attack on mediums.

Ford told Beal that he had a message for him from his dead father. The medium said the father spoke of a letter he once had written to his son when the latter was a boy, and he quoted these three lines from it:

"God bless your little heart. I send you a million XXXXX. With love to my boy. Pa."

Taken aback, Beal refused to acknowledge that the message was evidential. Ford told him to "check it out."

Beal searched for his father's letter, which he thought had been destroyed, and when he found it was astonished to discover that the last three lines were exactly as Ford had given them. Even the number of X's—five—was correct.

In Arthur Ford's personal papers I found a letter from Joseph Carlton Beal in which he said:

"Your message on Sunday night at Jordan Hall was not only startling—it was uncanny.

"The information you gave was known to nobody but my dead father and myself."

Arthur Ford claimed that the information had come from Beal's dead father. However, it might have been plucked telepathically from Beal's own unconscious mind.

Message from the dead? Or mind reading?

67. The Mystery That Perplexed Dunninger

Remember that master of mystery, Dunninger?

During the 1940's and 1950's he was the biggest name among the show-business mind readers. On his network radio program, and later on a top-rated weekly television show, he electrified audiences by his apparent ability to probe their innermost thoughts.

The master "mentalist"—Dunninger claims to have invented that word—lived, until his recent death, in virtual seclusion in Cliffside, New Jersey, in a house jammed with mementos of his colorful career. Before his death, he granted a rare interview to a friend of mine, the Reverend Canon William V. Rauscher of Woodbury, New Jersey, an Episcopal priest noted for his investigations of ESP and related phenomena.

In the interview Dunninger admitted that though he used gimmicks to put on a good show, not everything was a trick. Sometimes things happened that baffled even him.

Let's recall a typical Dunninger television program in the 1950's.

Dunninger was introduced by the announcer as "the man who does the impossible." He strode from the wings—a tall, imposing figure in a blue serge suit and maroon tie, with a flowing mane of gray hair. His presence was commanding, almost hypnotic in its effect on the audience.

"Ladies and gentlemen," he intoned in a resonant voice with an ever-so-slight British accent, "my work here tonight is legitimate. Yes, I really can tune in upon your minds, but only if you help me—only if you concentrate. I am not psychic. I make no supernatural claims. I depend upon your concentration."

Then Dunninger sat down on a chair on the stage, removed a small pad from his righthand coat pocket, and flourished it to show that it was blank. He wrote on the pads.

"I am receiving an impression from someone in the studio audience," he said. "I get the impression of the word 'Tiger.' Does that mean anything to anyone?"

A well-dressed lady arose and acknowledged that it did.

"Madam," said Dunninger in a ringing voice, "we have never spoken to each other?"

"No," the lady replied firmly.

"You pledge your word of honor we have never met before or prearranged anything?"

"Yes," she replied with feeling.

"Very well. Tell me, what is 'Tiger'?"

"It's my maiden name," said the lady.

"And what would the name Greer be?"

"That's my married name."

"And who is Almon?" Dunninger asked.

"My husband."

"And Fern?"

"My daughter."

Dunninger said, "Thank you, madam," and the lady, obviously stunned, sat down amid wild applause.

Was Dunninger really a mind reader? Well, that's a difficult question to answer. Many knowledgeable people say no, that all his effects could be produced by trickery. Dunninger acknowledged to Canon Rauscher, "I use any means necessary to please and impress my audience."

But occasionally, he said, strange things happened that perplexed even him, such as one eerie incident in particular.

"Several days after the assassination of President Kennedy I was giving a performance in Dallas," Dunninger recalled.

"The auditorium was packed with some 3,000 people. The audience was so large that they sat on the sides of the platform—it wasn't a stage—and could even see in back of me, which I didn't mind.

"I gave my usual performance of thought reading, using the note pad. Suddenly, a streak of red, like red paint, about an inch wide and six inches long, appeared on the note pad. It was wet, and in the shape of a crescent moon.

"I looked to see if my finger was bleeding but it wasn't. The audience on the side saw the thing too and looked at one another. I didn't know what it was.

"I tore off the page, put it on the table to inspect it later, and went on with the show. Afterward I was mobbed by people, and by the time I looked for the page the caretakers had already thrown it in the garbage along with all the other surplus stuff on the platform.

"Then I discovered that President Kennedy had sat in the very chair I had used, a few nights before—on the eve of his assassination."

68. The Woman Who Makes Objects Dance for Her

Can the human will, without employing any physical agency, move objects?

Recently I saw a Soviet-made scientific film of an experiment with a Leningrad housewife named Nelya Mikhailova. The experiment was designed to test whether this plump, fortyish woman could, as she claimed, make objects move by willpower alone.

In the film Mrs. Mikhailova sat at a small table on which were scattered a number of objects—a magnetic compass, a bunch of matchsticks, several cigarettes, an empty wine glass.

Seated beside the woman was the Soviet scientist who arrange the experiment, Dr. Leonid Vasiliev, now deceased, a leading authority in parapsychology (the science of psychic phenomena).

Hunching over the table and crinkling her brow in concentration, Mrs. Mikhailova began passing her hands back and forth, in rhythmic gestures, the needle reversed the direction of its spin.

Then the cigarettes rolled across the table, sometimes individually, sometimes in a group. Next, the matchsticks wriggled this way and that. And finally the wine glass glided across the table toward her, and so on, several times.

A trick you say? Well, not surprisingly, this possibility occurred to those investigating Mrs. Mikhailova. However, the more than 40 Soviet scientists who have studied her, including two Nobel prize winners, insist that hidden wires, threads, or other such gimmicks cannot explain Mrs. Mikhailova's unusual performances.

She has moved objects which were covered by a plastic dome, thus apparently ruling out the use of wires.

Dr. Ya Tertlesky, chairman of Moscow University's department of theoretical physics, said flatly: "Mrs. Mikhailova, we are certain, displays a new and unknown form of energy."

Mind you, not everybody is convinced. An attack on Mrs. Mikhailova in *Pravda*, the official Soviet government newspaper, called her a fraud who manipulates the objects with the aid of tiny magnets hidden on her person. If you ask how magnets could move a wooden object such as a matchstick, there are ways—an ordinary metal pin inserted into the matchstick, for example.

The defenders of the mind-over-matter woman cite significant indirect evidence of her genuineness. When she is trying to move objects her pulse reportedly increases to 250—three times the normal rate—indicating that she is exerting tremendous effort.

And in some cases, Mrs. Mikhailova is said to have lost as much as three pounds during a demonstration.

69. How to Become Psychic—By Falling on Your Head

One of the most curious of all the curious things about extrasensory perception is the way it's often triggered by a physical or mental shock.

Edgar Cayce, the famed Sleeping Prophet, as a child was knocked out by a baseball; it was after this, apparently, that he developed his mysterious powers.

The noted psychic Peter Hurkos, when he was 20, fell off a ladder, lobotomizing himself (technically, he suffered lesions of the pineal, hypothalamus, and brain stem areas) and woke up in hospital a mind reader.

D. D. Home, the great nineteenth-century medium who called up the dead in some of Europe's most fashionable drawing rooms (including those of the French and Russian courts) had his first vision when he was 13; it followed the sudden death of his best friend, a boy named Edwin.

Ronald Edwin, a contemporary English psychic, unequivocally attributes his own ability to see "spirits" to having fallen on his head as a child.

And in 1967, a Vermont high school girl named Lyse Savard told a court in Montpelier that since a three-ton truck crashed into her house she had been able to see and communicate with the dead; she brought suit against the owner of the truck for having made her an involuntary medium.

Possibly the most remarkable case in which trauma appears to have unleashed unusual creativity was that of Minou

Drouet, who a few years ago became famous as a child poet.

In 1953 Minou Drouet was a little French girl, six years old, and mentally very average. In fact, she was considered to be, as we now say, a slow learner. Certainly there appears to have been nothing exceptional or surprising about her in the least.

Then she developed a form of encephalitis—brain fever. She lapsed into a deep coma and wasn't expected to live. If she did survive, the doctors feared that she would have irreversible brain damage.

When Minou Drouet awakened from the coma, she had become a different person.

How different?

Well, she sat down and wrote a poem (in French, of course) which began: "My heart is an empty boat whose harbor is nowhere."

Does that sound like the average six-year-old?

Skeptics suggested that Minou was a fake and somebody else wrote the poems. French writer Jean Cocteau said she wasn't really a child but an 80-year-old dwarf.

However, Minou Drouet's authenticity was proven when a committee of distinguished French scholars, as a test, assigned her a subject and she promptly wrote a poem about it.

Again, in December, 1956, when she was 10, she appeared on British television and during the 40-minute program wrote a poem on a subject assigned to her after the program started. The poem, entitled "London," began with these words: "London, my fingers have turned your pages like a disturbing fairy tale . . ."

Minou Drouet published two books of her collected poems and critics in both Britain and France hailed her as a literary prodigy.

And there were those who thought she was more than just a poet. British critic Peter Quennell suggested that Minou Drouet was "an uncommonly gifted medium who picks up the ideas relayed to her from a far more complex brain."

Curiously, Minou herself said her poems came to her from a mysterious realm she called "the otherwhere."

Why should physical or mental shock sometimes trigger psychic or creative abilities?

One theory is that a blow on the head such as Peter Hurkos had may shuffle or rearrange a person's neural circuits—somewhat as wires in a telephone exchange can become crossed—and thereby change an ordinary person into a psychic. Similarly, a very high fever, as in Minou Drouet's case, may cause something in the brain analogous to the fusing of wires at extremely high temperatures.

Maybe the best we can say is that it's part of the unexplained ...

70. Luck or Psi?

A man who prides himself on his punctuality is late for work the morning a mad gunman shoots up his office, killing several employees.

A businessman impulsively unloads a stock that's been doing very well and the next day it plunges out of sight.

Or, less dramatic, a writer who's going crazy trying to find a quotation he needs picks up a book that drops open at that very quotation.

Coincidence? Luck? Or do such incidents represent something more?

Dr. Rex Stanford thinks there may be something more. And, says this University of Virginia parapsychologist, the something more could be "unconscious psi"—psi (pronounced "sigh") being a technical term for ESP and related phenomena.

Some people, he suggests, may exert an unsuspected influence over the events in their lives by a psychic force they generate without knowing it.

This would explain why certain individuals seem to attract good luck while others can't win even at solitaire. In Dr. Stanford's theory, the ones with good luck have powerful unconscious psi working for them.

He cites some pertinent cases to illustrate his point.

"A 15-year-old girl, phoning her cousin, misdialed the number and reached a 75-year-old lady who was having a heart attack and was alone at the time. She cried out for help over the phone and then collapsed.

"The girl had the call traced, and an ambulance rushed the heart attack victim to the hospital, no doubt saving her life."

Did the teen-ager dial the wrong number—or the right number—by mistake? Or was she, unawares, responding to a psychic call-for-help from the elderly woman? For the latter, it certainly was no mistake but a miracle.

In another incident, a man was called, quite accidentally, as a witness in an armed robbery case about which he knew nothing. The police said that he had been called by mistake. However, he recognized the defendant in the case as the same man who two months earlier had robbed him of $1,000 and escaped.

In still another case, a 21-year-old man known to Dr. Stanford was one of six youth advisors participating in the annual Selective Service lottery in Washington, D.C., on February 2, 1972—a ritual to decide the fate of thousands of young men subject to the draft.

From the drum he picked his own brother's birthdate which matched the lucky number—343—drawn simultaneously by another person from a different drum. This meant his brother would not be drafted. The odds against such a coincidence are astronomical.

Was it a coincidence, or, as Dr. Stanford wonders, is unconscious psi involved in such cases?

When that witness turned up in the courtroom by accident, was it really an accident? Or a trap devised by his unconscious psi to catch the thief?

And did the young man pick that one-in-a-million number by sheer blind luck or by his unconscious psychic ability?

Dr. Stanford points out that in all these cases some human need was met by the curious coincidence and suggests that the need may have created the coincidence.

But wait a minute. If we assume, for the sake of argument, that unconscious psi is a fact, and that we are, unawares, shaping our own everyday lives, wouldn't it work negatively too?

Couldn't some people use their psi for self-defeating purposes—like the born loser who seems to have a will to fail, or the man who has continual accidents presumably because he hates himself?

Come to think of it, what was the real reason my car wouldn't start this morning?

71. A Mentalist Squeals on All the Others

The famous radio and television mind reader of 20 years ago, Dunninger, shortly before his death wrote a book in which he told how his rival mentalists perform their bogus miracles.

All other mind readers, says Dunninger (in *Dunninger's Secrets*, written with Walter Gibson), including the current favorite Kreskin, are fakes. Dunninger himself? Well, he's different, he says.

Besides revealing how Kreskin bamboozles audiences with his phony ESP, Dunninger (who during the 1940's and 1950's was as popular as his younger rival is now) takes a few swipes at his friend, the late great Harry Houdini. Dunninger pictures Houdini as a rather dumb vaudeville escape artist whose word was not always to be trusted.

Dunninger and Houdini were friendly rivals during the heyday of stage magic in the 1920's. That was also the era when Houdini boosted sagging box offices by making a name for himself as an exposer of fake mediums (in addition to escaping from anything—handcuffs, straitjackets, and jail cells).

But, says Dunninger, Houdini was not always telling the truth when he claimed to have caught a medium in trickery. Sometimes he claimed to know how a medium produced a certain psychic phenomenon when he actually had no idea how the trick (if it was a trick) was done.

As an example, Dunninger tells how he once did some mind reading for Houdini in the latter's office. Dunninger claims that he was able to read some of the contents of letters on Houdini's desk without touching them. Houdini explained it by saying that Dunninger had simply read the words backwards through the thin paper while he (Houdini) held each letter up to scan it.

Dunninger scoffs at Houdini's explanation. How, then, did he do it? Well, he insists it was for real—that unlike the other phonies in the business he can read minds. That, Houdini never accepted.

For his part, Dunninger mocks any suggestion that his present successor, Kreskin, is genuinely psychic.

"The bulk of his program," Dunninger says of Kreskin, "is made up of items that the average cub scout could acquire from any well-equipped magic shop. Yet this self-appointed mastermind has the effrontery to appear on television and present such stuff under the guise of 'miracles.'"

Explaining how Kreskin performs some of his wonders, Dunninger says that any feat involving cards is based on a trick deck. He describes these in detail, naming some of them, and showing how any number of seemingly impossible psychic wonders are possible with them. They can all be purchased from a magic supply store.

Dunninger refers to one performance in which Kreskin demonstrated his ability to see without eyes. Blindfolded, "He went groping around the studio using some secret sense to track down a large toy balloon that a spectator was holding on a string.

"Finally getting his bearings, the Mighty Marvel bore down upon his prey, made a dramatic gesture with a long pin that he carried, and stabbed the balloon so perfectly that it went pow! Then he informed the rapt viewers that another miracle had been achieved in the name of science and ESP."

The truth, says Dunninger, is simply that Kreskin could see through the blindfold. Trick blindfolds, good enough to fool almost anyone, are a dime a dozen at your friendly magic store, he says.

"It never occurred to anyone to ask," he adds, "why the Mighty Marvel, who claimed the ability to find tiny objects hidden almost anywhere, needed an inflated balloon as a target when working blindfolded.

"The reason was that he couldn't see anything smaller without his glasses. If he had worn them under his blindfold, the act would have looked even funnier than it was."

So now Dunninger, the man who claims to have invented the word "mentalist," has debunked all his rivals as mere showmen and tricksters.

Question: Who now is going to believe that Dunninger is any different from the rest?

72. The Medium They Couldn't Fool

David Young is the medium they couldn't fool.

"They" in this case refers to a squad of investigative reporters assigned by the British newspaper *News of the World* to test the genuineness of some well-known mediums.

Can mediums, as they claim, establish communication with the dead? Or do they merely fish for information, which the sitter unwittingly gives them, and then hand it back as a message from the departed?

To find out, *News of the World* told several reporters to assume false identities and arrange sittings with 10 prominent London mediums.

"Our reporters all had the same instructions," said the newspaper. "If the medium takes the initiative with honest and accurate information, be yourself."

"But if you are asked questions, or the medium takes you through a list of common names asking if you know a Fred or Mabel in spirit, think yourself into your prepared false identity."

For nine of the mediums the results were embarrassing. Each took the bait and obligingly gave the reporter communications from a nonexistent Uncle Harry or Aunt Bess. Evidently the mediums "spirit guides" were not able to distinguish fact from fiction.

One medium, Marie Wheeler, gave reporter Sue Kentish a stream of supposedly personal information which was totally wrong, said *News of the World*. "Then she brought in 17 different spirits, including a cat, none of which the reporters recognized."

When the same reporter had a sitting with a medium named Jordan Gill, she planted the false idea she had a baby son in the spirit world.

"Immediately, Mr. Gill gave a detailed description of his nonexistent dead child and said, 'He is standing by your side. He is holding a bunch of violets for you.' "

However, one medium out of the 10 confounded the skeptics—and they admitted it. He was 27-year-old David Young, whose psychic demonstrations I have had the opportunity to observe.

This is how reporter Michael Cable described his encounter with Young:

"I had my fictitious story ready but I didn't get the chance to tell it.

"Very early in the sitting Young gave me some family details which were accurate. He seemed more anxious to tell me things than to pry information out of me.

"I came away impressed because he gave character assessments of members of my family which were very similar to my own impressions of those relatives.

"Young did seem to know an amazing amount of what was in my mind."

Whether the medium's performance indicated communication with the dead or mind reading is debatable. However, it did suggest something more than guesswork.

Sometimes David Young performs feats which seem positively uncanny.

In 1972, while visiting Vancouver, he was a guest on the phone-in radio show of Pat Burns, Canada's high priest of the "hot line." Burns, a tough, hardnosed skeptic who has debunked his share of phonies, himself told me what happened.

Out of the blue, David Young mentioned that the gold ring on Burns's finger was his deceased mother's wedding band, and Burns acknowledged that this was so. The medium then asked if Burns were aware of an inscription inside the ring, and the reply was no.

Well, said the medium, there was such an inscription, and Pat Burns's mother, as evidence of her survival, was going to reveal it. The medium proceeded, with some faltering, to spell out the word "LANBRO."

A quick glance by Pat Burns inside the ring confirmed that there was indeed an inscription but too small for him to read. However, with a borrowed jeweler's lens he could clearly see the word "LANBRO."

The jeweler said that no doubt this was the name of the goldsmith who made the ring in Ireland some 50 years ago.

How did David Young know that inscription?

73. Do Objects Have a Memory?

The idea that an object such as a comb, a pipe, or a watch has "memories" may seem absurd. But . . .

Dr. J.N. Emerson, professor of archeology at the University of Toronto, says he has scientific evidence that either objects do have some sort of "memory" (for want of a better word) or something even more bizarre is going on. At any rate, he says, some people can, merely by handling an object, discover facts about its history which they could not possibly know by normal means.

Dr. Emerson describes the feats of a "psychic informant" who wishes to be known only as George.

"I presented George with a fragment of an Indian artifact excavated from a site located near Toronto," said the professor.

"He held the fragment in his hand, contemplated it, fondled it, and meditated upon it at length.

"He then correctly told me that it was a pipe stem, told me the age of the site where it was found, the location of the site, described how the pipe was manufactured, described the maker, and provided details about the community and the living conditions. He then took a piece of paper in hand and drew a picture of the pipe bowl which he said belonged on the broken pipe stem.

"I was fascinated and impressed. He had drawn a picture of a typical Iroquois conical ring bowl pipe, as it's called by archeologists."

Could George simply have guessed?

Dr. Emerson doesn't think so. He describes George as a man with "a minimum of formal education" who rarely reads anything and appears to know virtually nothing about the culture of the North American Indian except what he has seen on television.

Well, did George read the archeologist's mind?

Dr. Emerson remarks that this would be quite a feat in itself, but it doesn't explain George's power because sometimes he correctly picks up information unknown to the scientist.

In one case, Dr. Emerson received a letter from a woman containing an old coin. The woman asked if George could tell her anything about the coins. She had mailed it from the Ontario town of Markstay, a small community with which Dr. Emerson was unfamiliar. He had no idea where Markstay was located in the province.

However, after George had handled the coin (which was of George III vintage and could have come from anywhere) Dr. Emerson asked him where it was found.

"Sudbury," he said immediately, "North Bay, Callender."

These are the names of three towns in the same approximate area of Northern Ontario. When Dr. Emerson checked the atlas, he found that Markstay was located 20 miles east of Sudbury and 60 miles west of North Bay and Callender.

There was another case in which George couldn't have been reading his mind, said Dr. Emerson, since they disagreed on the matter at issue.

George and the archeologist visited a prehistoric Iroquois village site near Peterborough, Ontario, and the psychic said emphatically that the villagers there had not cultivated corn, beans, or squash. Dr. Emerson disagreed since these three crops were traditional to Iroquois farming. Moreover, digging at the site had turned up plenty of evidence of beans, squash, and corn seeds.

It looked as though George was proven wrong but he still insisted the villagers had not cultivated those crops.

However, a very careful study of the soil showed no evidence of pollen belonging to the three vegetables George had specified. It appeared that the villagers had obtained these vegetables by trade with their neighbors and had not themselves grown them—exactly as George said.

George is not infallible, Dr. Emerson is quick to note. He has his off days.

"But on an archeological site he almost quivers and comes alive like a senstive bird dog scenting the prey," the scientist adds.

And, strangest of all, the "scent" George picks up comes not from the present but from the past . . .

74. The Amazing Mr. Croiset

He looks not unlike the popular image of a psychic—a man in his fifties, with large staring eyes and hair like an explosion in a Brillo factory.

But Gerard Croiset, make no mistake, is not a mere show biz "mind reader" nor some phony medium who conjures up spooks in dark rooms. Ask the police departments that have used his help or the scientists who've studied him.

Croiset, who lives in Utrecht, Holland, where I met him recently, has worked closely for years with a respected scientist, Dr. W.H.C. Tenhaeff, professor of parapsychology at the University of Utrecht. It is Tenhaeff who has documented most of Croiset's uncanny feats. And, significantly, neither man has made a penny from this research.

Croiset's greatest claim to fame is his ability to track missing persons, from an article of the individuals clothing or a photograph. Police forces in Europe and the U.S. have acknowledged receiving his help.

In the January, 1962, issue of Holland's official police journal, *Tijdschrift de Politie*, this Croiset case was reported.

On August 8, 1961, a Dutch boy, 7-year-old Jurrien van Dijkhuizen, disappeared from his home in the town of Nijkerk. Croiset, without being told the boy's name nor his town, was asked for help. His "impressions" were tape-recorded by the police adjutant, J.H. Lovink.

The psychic gave a remarkably accurate description of the boy's neighborhood and concluded with: "Water and reeds are nearby, and heaps of sand. In that area the child has drowned."

The next day the boy's body was found in the water where he had drowned, amid the reeds with heaps of sand close by.

Even more uncanny than Croiset's radar brain is his apparent ability to break the time barrier. Consider his famous "chair-tests."

The procedure for these is simple: Croiset is given several randomly selected seat numbers for some specific future event—a lecture, play or concert—and, before the event, tapes his descriptions of the individuals who will occupy those seats.

Unlike professional mentalists, with Croiset there is no hanky-panky about the predictions being made secretly and played only after the event—there are two dozen tricks for doing this, and I know most of them. In contrast, Croiset's descriptions are witnessed by scientists when he makes them.

Impossible? Of course it is. But what happens?

Well, here are some results of such a chair test conducted in Denver by a group of scientists, including Dr. Jule Eisenbud, associate professor of psychiatry at the University of Colorado medical school.

On January 6, 1969, Croiset, who was in Utrecht, taped his descriptions of several people who were to be selected randomly at a meeting in Denver some three weeks later. The descriptions were translated into English by Dr. Tenhaeff and sent to Dr. Eisenbud long before the night of the experiment.

On January 23, at 8 P.M., about 100 people assembled in the International House, Denver, on a first-come first-served basis. Forty of them were given tickets numbered 1 to 40.

Then numbers were randomly drawn, and in each case Croiset's description of that particular individual was read. There were some astonishing hits. A few examples from Dr. Eisenbud's detailed report:

"The person who drew the first number is a lady about 5 feet 6 inches tall," said Croiset.

The first person was a woman 5 feet 6 inches tall.

"She is dark haired or wears a dark beret."

The women's hair is dark and her hairstyle, which she hasn't changed in years, has been described as looking like a beret.

"She recently pressed her nose so hard into a window before which she was standing as to almost go through it."

The woman said that a month earlier she had been standing before the observation window in the hospital trying to catch a glimpse of her newborn grandson when "I ducked forward and bumped my nose quite severely on the glass."

"The lady," said Croiset, "recently experienced some emotion connected with page 64 of a book."

She had been quite upset, the women said, reading a book entitled *The Cat You Care For,* when she came to a section on how to put your pet to sleep. This reminded her of when she had had to destroy a much loved cat. The section proved to be on page 64 of the book

How does Croiset do it?

Reputable scientists believe he demonstrates that the human mind can, on occasion, unchain itself from both space and time.

75. The Not-So-Amazing World of Kreskin

Kreskin, the stage and television mentalist, has written a book called *The Amazing World of Kreskin*. I suggest it be retitled, *The Not-So-Amazing World of Kreskin*.

It's not so amazing if you know the gimmicks that mentalists and other pseudo-psychics use to perform their marvels. Since Kreskin in his book criticizes "mediums," "seers," and other so-called phonies, it is only fitting that we should critically examine what he himself and his fellow mentalists do.

In a nutshell: Kreskin is about as psychic as an oyster.

Virtually anybody, with the intelligence of a normal 12-year-old and armed with the necessary tricks purchased from the magic supply house, can do what the Kreskins do. Let's examine a few of his "amazing" feats and see just how amazing they aren't.

Kreskin claims to be able to "read" peoples thoughts. He implies that he does this by ESP.

One guest on Kreskin's TV show (which is taped in Ottawa, Ontario) was Dr. William Taylor, director of Canada's National Museum of Man. He was asked to bring to the show, wrapped securely, a sample from the museum. What he brought was a fragment of an ivory comb 6000 years old.

"I didn't tell anybody what I was bringing," he said, "not my wife or my secretary or anybody at the studio. I wanted to fool Kreskin."

He didn't. Kreskin gazed upon Taylor and the box and told him and a suitably astonished audience exactly what was in the box and how old it was. The scientist was convinced Kreskin had read his mind.

However, watching the show, I turned to my wife and said: "The old clipboard trick." Later, a call to Dr. Taylor confirmed my suspicion.

The trick, you see, is simple. You can purchase it from

magic supply shops for $35.00. It consists of an ordinary looking clipboard, such as college students use to take notes in class. But the hard top is carboned and gives the mentalist an exact copy of anything written on the clipboard.

My conversation with Dr. Taylor revealed that yes, Kreskin had asked him to write down the contents of the sealed box before the show, but no, he wasn't suspicious because he kept the piece of paper and Kreskin even left the room while he wrote on it. Of course, all the mentalist had to do was return later and retrieve the clipboard for a copy of what had been written.

Kreskin's other wonders can be similarly explained. On one show he had actor William Shatner, once of *Star Trek*, locked in chains. There were 10 keys, all of which had been tested by members of the studio to show that only one, the last key that was tried, would open the locks. Then all the keys were put into a bowl and Kreskin went out of the television studio to a phone booth.

Inside the studio, members of the audience came on stage, took a key each from the bowl and stood in line. From the phone booth outside, Kreskin called and picked a number signifying which one in the lineup had the key that would unlock Shatner's chains. The key opened the lock.

ESP? No, a trick lock.

It can be purchased from magic supply shops (such as Lou Tannen's in New York, where they told a friend of mine, the Reverend William Rauscher, and myself that Kreskin was a customer) for about $10.00. The key that opens the lock the first time triggers a mechanism in the lock which enables all the other keys to open it. The mentalist can't lose. Later, he resets the lock and its ready for the stunt to be repeated.

What about predicting the future?

Kreskin claims to have predicted newspaper headlines. The "prediction" is locked in a box, the box is opened 24 hours later, and the written headline proves to match the actual headline. Meanwhile the mentalist has had direct physical contact with the box.

It looks good but the gimmick is the key that opens the box. The key a large, elaborate affair, is hollow and contains a spring mechanism. The correct prediction (written after the newspaper is published) is loaded into the key and the act of turning it in the lock propels the rolled-up piece of paper inside it into the box.

Mentalism is great fun. As entertainment, I love it. But when a mentalist such as Kreskin claims (as he does in his book) that he's using ESP—well, that's something else.

76. The Girl Who Dreamed Her Death

In July, 1973, the Reverend Canon William V. Rauscher heard of the funeral service of a 13-year-old girl who had died tragically.

Canon Rauscher, rector of Christ Episcopal Church in Woodbury, New Jersey, learned after the funeral that six months earlier the girl had dreamed her death.

In the dream she died from "a freak accident." In reality, she died after a tractor trailer jumped the curb and crushed her while she walked with her mother near her home. (The mother suffered a broken pelvis in the accident.)

Let's call the girl (whose mother wishes anonymity) Judy. Shortly after Judy's death a friend gave her mother a letter the dead girl had written on December 6, 1972. The letter was eerily prophetic.

Judy wrote to her friend that she dreamed she had been injured in an accident and lay in hospital near death.

"The doctors said I had only a 30 percent chance of recovery," the girl wrote.

She described a procession of high school friends who visited her. And, then, in the dream, she died.

"From somewhere above me I heard a voice," she wrote, "which said 'Judy Jones died from a freak accident at the age of 13.

" 'She had many friends who loved her and still love her now, even though she is no longer with us. They think of her often. When they think of her, they do not think of her untimely death but her short but fulfilled and happy life.' "

Then, in her dream, Judy said she saw and heard a friend telling a group of her classmates:

" 'I hope that you will not remember Judy by her death but by her simply super life. And tonight when you pray to God, remember to ask him to help us remember Judy.' "

The letter concluded: "Then the dream ended. Do you think it could be true? Love, Judy ..."

Six months later Judy was dead.

Of this experience Canon Rauscher said, "The letter is deeply moving to read. It is hard not to believe that Judy really did, in some mysterious way, glimpse what lay ahead for her—death at such an early age, victim of a freak accident.

"Yet this incident is not depressing but inspiring. It has a spiritual quality. It reminds us that we live surrounded by mystery but the most profound and wonderful mystery of all is the human spirit which transcends time and space and even death."

77. Clairvoyant Tracks a Missing Girl

One of the objections brought against many so-called clairvoyants is that the statements motivated by their psychic powers are usually trivial. There is some justification for this charge.

However, there are cases in which a clairvoyant has provided information useful to the police in solving a crime or other mystery. And at least one such case was vouched for by a policeman.

The officer was Robert Finch, police chief of Boardman Township, Ohio, in 1963. The case that baffled him was the disappearance of a 17-year-old girl named Carol Allen.

The girl vanished on the night of August 5, 1963. She was last seen getting into the car of a young married man whom she had dated several times.

The man, under police questioning, admitted that he and Carol had planned to go to California and start a new life together. But he had changed his mind, he said, and decided to turn back. There was a quarrel and the girl got out of the car.

The spot where Carol Allen left the car was said to have been on Ohio State Highway 40 near the Indiana border.

An intensive police search turned up no trace of the missing girl. Every lead ended in a blind alley.

Then, in November, 1964—more than a year after the girl

vanished—Police Chief Finch found himself doing something that made him feel foolish. He was on his way to Edgewater, New Jersey, to see a clairvoyant named Florence Sternfels. (Mrs. Sternfels has since died.)

Chief Finch said he had been talked into going, against his better judgment, by the missing girl's mother who had heard of Mrs. Sternfels and hoped she might be able to provide a clue.

Totally skeptical, Chief Finch said he checked with the police in Edgewater, New Jersey, and found, to his surprise, that they spoke respectfully of Mrs. Sternfels and said she had been consulted by more than one police force across the country.

In the interview Chief Finch had with Mrs. Sternfels, she held a locket belonging to the missing girl. There was a long silence as the clairvoyant appeared to be deep in concentration. Then she made some flat declarations which shook the policeman.

The missing girl was alive and well, she said. Furthermore, Chief Finch himself would be talking to her within two weeks.

The officer left, shaking his head and wondering why he had ever bothered to consult a clairvoyant in the first place. Her prediction seemed—well, absurd, to put it politely.

But what happened?

On November 21, 1964, two weeks after the interview with Mrs. Sternfels, Chief Finch discovered that Carol Allen, the missing girl, had written to a friend back home in Ohio. He phoned the girl at her new address in California.

She told Chief Finch that she had traveled to California on her own, met a nice young man, married, and become a mother. She apologized for any trouble she unwittingly had caused her family and the police.

And so the case had a happy ending.

But it also ended with a mystery.

How did Florence Sternfels know that Carol Allen was alive and well and that Police Chief Robert Finch would be talking to her in two weeks' time?

PART V

Mysteries of Ghosts and Messages from the Dead

78. Clocks With a Mind of Their Own

Thomas Alva Edison, the great inventor, died at 3:24 A.M., Sunday October 18, 1931.

In his laboratory office, three minutes after his death, a large 30-day wall clock stopped. Three of Edison's top executives noticed that their clocks also stopped at 3:24 A.M.

The night watchman at the Edison Laboratory, where the inventor had his office, John Flanagan, told Edison's son that certainly he had not stopped the clock. And the three executives could offer no explanation as to why their clocks should each have stopped at the same time as Edison's death.

Could more than coincidence have been involved?

Some of the inventor's friends and associates wondered about this in view of Edison's great fondness for the song, "My Grandfather's Clock," which he had had recorded on both cylinder and disks. The song said:

> It (the clock) was bought on the morn
> Of the day he was born
> And was always his treasure and pride;
> But it stopped short, never to go again,
> When the old man died . . .

There was an added curious link between Thomas Edison and this song—his employees and associated always called him "The Old Man."

There are numerous instances of unexplained clock-stopping at the time of a person's death.

When the first president of the American Society for Psychical Research, Professor James Hyslop, died, his daughter's watch stopped at the same moment. Later, Hyslop's secretary, Gertrude Tubby, who knew nothing about the watch stopping, received through a medium a message purportedly from Hyslop that he had affected his daughter's watch as a sign of his continued existence.

In 1966, Terry Allen of Indio, California, went to Vietnam with the U.S. Army. Before leaving, he bought his mother a wall clock for her kitchen.

The clock ticked away uneventfully for five months. Then, on May 5, 1967, at 2:10 P.M., it inexplicably stopped. A few days later a telegram came saying that Private First Class Terry J. Allen of the Ninth Infantry Division had been killed on patrol in the Mekong Delta.

The young man's death occurred on the date—and, so far as his parents were able to determine, at the time—the gift clock stopped.

After the suicide of the son of the late Bishop James Pike—formerly Episcopal bishop of California—the alarm clock belonging to the younger Pike was found to have stopped at 8:19. This was the approximate time of the junior Pike's death.

A woman in Chicago, reported her experience to a noted parapsychologist, Dr. Louisa Rhine.

"The day of Mother's death in 1952, the clock stopped at the exact time of her passing. I rewound the clock and the next day it stopped again at that exact time. It has never since stopped at that time."

I had a personal experience with a clock which seemed to show a mind of its own.

My father died on Monday January 6, 1964. It was 4:30 A.M. when the hospital phoned with the news that he had passed away a short time before.

From my father's apartment I took home an old alarm clock which my parents had had for some 20 years, though I couldn't recall their ever having used the alarm on it. This clock was put on a shelf in our kitchen. It sat there for several days, behaving itself.

Then, on Sunday night—one week after my father's death—the clock suddenly started buzzing, waking my wife and me from a sound sleep. We discovered that the alarm—which I had not touched—was set at 4:30. The alarm had gone off, in other words, exactly one week after the news of my father's death had come to us.

As my wife remarked, "Who would ever set an alarm for a time like that?"

A clock, when you think about it, isn't a bad symbol of mortality. And the unexplained stopping of a clock could be interpreted as signifying a dimension where time is no more.

Or, of course, it could be sheer coincidence.

79. The Ghost of Mullica Hill

Does a ghost—whatever that is—have a smell?

Yes, it's a crazy question. But according to the Rev. Harry Collins and his wife Joan the answer is yes.

And they speak from experience.

They live, with their three children, in the vicarage of St. Stephen's Episcopal Church in Mullica Hill, a small New Jersey town where Father Collins is a parish priest. Ever since they moved into the house in August, 1969, peculiar things have happened.

"Nothing much at first," Joan Collins told me. "We noticed that the tablecloth in the dining room was folded back, accordion-style, when none of us had done it.

"This happened repeatedly when my husband and I were out and the children were asleep, or when we were all asleep, or when we were all out and the house was empty and locked up.

"Then we frequently found the end cushion on the sofa moved into a position which suggested somebody had been sleeping and using it as a pillow. For a while I shrugged this off as probably being due to our two cats. But after the cats left, it continued."

There was a year and a half of these unspectacular but nonetheless puzzling incidents before Act Two started.

The inexplicable smells came.

"We noticed a strong aroma pervading parts of the house," said Father Collins. "It was a spicy, pleasant odor, hard to identify.

"Besides my wife and I, our 15-year-old son smelled it and he suggested, 'It's like one of those mosquito candles.'

"This was significant. Previously my wife and I had agreed between ourselves that the smell was like citronella, which of course is a mosquito repellent. Not an identical smell but close to it."

The smell was localized in the living room and dining room. The Collinses speculated that possibly humidity was releasing odors from the plaster of the walls. But then another, quite different smell came.

"This one is so strong there's no mistaking it," said Joan Collins. "It smells like coffee perking and bacon cooking. It seems to come from the kitchen and waft through the whole house."

The odd phenomena reached a climax when Harry Collins saw—well, let him tell it.

"The date was March 6, 1971. Another couple had dropped in for a visit in the evening and we were all in the kitchen when I looked up and saw it standing in the hallway leading to the dining room.

"It was the figure of a man. He had muddy blond hair but his features were indistinct, as though they were in shadow. He was wearing an Eisenhower jacket and his hands were shoved deep into the slit pockets.

"The figure was perfectly distinct and solid-looking down to the knees but below there it trailed off so that I could see the floorboards through where the legs should have been."

As the clergyman stared at the figure, dumbfounded, it faded away like a television image when the set is switched off. By the time he had alerted his companions, it was gone.

His reaction?

"I knew I had seen something uncanny but there was nothing threatening about it. I didn't feel a chill invade the room or anything like that."

Joan Collins' turn to meet the uninvited visitor came a year later.

"I was cleaning a downstairs closet one morning," she recalled, "when suddenly I felt what I can only describe as a sense of presence.

"I turned and found myself staring at the figure of a man no more than five feet from me. He looked so solid and lifelike that for an instant I thought he must be a flesh-and-blood intruder.

"He appeared to be in his early twenties, with light brown shaggy hair, wearing an Eisenhower jacket and military pants. The jacket and pants were a drab olive color.

"Suddenly he became transparent and just faded away."

Having no previous experience with ghosts, the Collinses are short on theories about who or what their unbidden guest is and why he is there. But they have grown rather to like him.

Theories, anybody?

80. The Sinister Tomb

In Barbados, a former burial vault has stood empty for more than a century because of its sinister reputation.

The dark chamber, 12 feet long, 6 feet wide, and high enough for a man to stand erect, is hewn out of solid limestone rock. It stands in the churchyard of Christ Church, Barbados, overlooking Ostin's Bay. At one time it served as a tomb for a family by the name of Chase.

Several accounts were written about the mystery of the Chase vault, the most detailed by the minister who served Christ Church for many years, the Reverend Thomas Orderson.

It was in 1807 that the first coffin was placed in the vault. From then until 1812 the chamber was opened twice to receive additional coffins. When it was opened a third time, later the same year, the first of a series of ominous discoveries was made.

The huge lead-lined coffins, one of which had taken eight men to carry, were strewn about the vault in crazy disorder. The coffins were straightened and the vault closed, this time being sealed with a massive stone slab put in place by four men.

Twice again the vault was opened for burials. Each time the coffins within were found in disarray—standing on end, lying across one another, upside down. They might have been tossed about by some giant in a mindless fury.

There was outrage at this apparent desecration of a resting place of the dead. But no evidence was found that anyone had tampered with the vault or its contents. And as for natural causes, there had been no earthquake, not even a tremor.

On July 17, 1819, Lord Combermere, governor of Barbados, presided at a solemn ceremony designed to prevent any further disturbance of the Chase vault. Another coffin was placed within, then sand was sprinkled thick on the floor, the tomb sealed, and a guard posted.

Almost a year later the chamber was reopened to admit

another coffin. Once more the coffins within were found scattered in wild confusion. Yet the seal on the entrance had not been broken, nor were any footprints visible in the sand sprinkled on the floor.

The coffins were removed and this time the dark chamber was left empty and so it has remained.

Whatever may dwell within now dwells alone ...

81. Know Any Live Vampires?

Raymond McNally is a professor with a somewhat unusual hobby—he's a vampirologist, a connoisseur of vampires. "If you hear of any living vampires I'd love to know about it," Dr. McNally said to me, straight-faced, when we met recently.

He explained that by living vampires he didn't mean reanimated corpses rising from their graves at night to plunder the blood of red-cheeked maidens. He meant human beings who because of some biochemical abnormality have literal craving for blood. "There have been such cases," the vampirologist assured me. "I know a doctor who's collecting cases for an article in one of the medical journals."

Raymond McNally has a Ph.D. in Russian history, the subject he teaches at Boston College. He looks, acts, and talks as a professor is supposed to look, act, and talk—except when he's discussing his passion for the living dead. How did an academic come by so exotic a second profession as vampirology?

"It started when I was a boy," McNally confessed. "I loved monster movies and stories."

His case became acute when he discovered that a colleague at Boston College, Radu Florescu, who teaches the Rumanian language and Balkan history, shared his passion for vampires and such. Being of Rumanian descent, Florescu had a particular interest in his legendary vampirical countryman, Count Dracula.

Florescu had a hunch that Dracula was more fact than fiction. He and McNally decided to investigate the Dracula legend. The result was their discovery of a flesh and blood historical monster that put the fictional one in the shade.

McNally and Florescu found that there was a real Prince (not Count) Dracula who ruled a part of Rumania in the fifteenth century and appears to have been, among other things, a homicidal maniac. He is reputed to have put to death some 100,000 people, many of them impaled on sharpened wooden spikes (hence, his grisly nickname, "The Impaler").

Transylvania, Dracula's homeland in novels and movies, is not (as some monster fans may have supposed) a mythical country but a real place, a province of Rumania. There is, still standing, an ancestral Castle Dracula, perched atop a precipice in the Transylvanian mountains.

In their on-the-spot research, McNally and Florescu found this castle. And they also encountered the Dracula curse.

"The people around the castle are very superstitious," McNally said. "When we asked for directions they said we must not go there, that the devil lived there guarding a treasure."

On the first attempt to reach the castle, Florescu's uncle, who was accompanying the two men, slipped and fell into a ravine, breaking his hip. The next time they made it to the castle, but upon entering it Florescu became violently ill. This he put down to nerves. McNally also had a curious experience. At one point he too suddenly became ill and fainted— not at Castle Dracula but when he found the evil prince's portrait in a gallery of monsters collected by a sixteenth-century Rumanian nobleman.

The researchers found that Dracula had been buried in the chapel of a monastery near Bucharest. From the time he was interred there, the monastery experienced a series of misfortunes, such as a freak accident in which an entire crowd of people perished. McNally and Florescu located Dracula's grave near the altar in the monastery chapel but it was empty, except for a few old bones which appeared to be of animal origin.

The vampirologists don't think the empty grave means Dracula is out looking for red-blooded victims, merely that his reputation was so sinister the monks quietly moved his body elsewhere.

Raymond McNally told me that even today in parts of Rumania, the vampire cult is very much alive. "In 1969," he said, "I was passing through the village of Rodna, near the Borgo Pass. I stopped to watch a burial taking place in the village graveyard. The bystanders told me that the deceased was a girl from the village who had died by suicide. The villagers were afraid that she would become a vampire after death. So they did what had to be done—and what I had read about for so many years. They plunged a stake through the heart of the corpse."

McNally is the author of a new book called *A Clutch of Vampires* (published by the New York Graphic Society) which he describes as "the most diversified collection of vampirana in English." There are accounts of historical vampires, excerpts from fiction, and a discussion of the movie treatments of the living dead.

The historical narratives include accounts by a first century Roman historian, a twelfth century bishop, a Cambridge philosopher in the 1600's, and a description of a vampire-hunt in a letter written in 1732 by an officer of the Austrian Imperial Army stationed in Southeastern Hungary.

In the letter, the officer gives this purported eyewitness account of the opening of the grave of a suspected vampire: "They found a sleek, fat corpse, as healthily colored as though the man were quietly and happily sleeping in calm repose. With a single blow from a sharp spade they cut off the head, whereupon there gushed forth a warm stream of blood filling the whole grave . . ."

Not all vampires hail from exotic places like Transylvania. One of those in McNally's book is an English representative of the blood-sucking breed fondly known to aficionados of the subject as the Croglin Grange Vampire.

In this charming tale (committed to paper by Augustus Hare in his *Story of My Life*) a family named Fisher, between 1680 and 1690, leased their manor house, Croglin Grange, to two brothers and their spinster sister. The first few months in the house passed uneventfully for the trio. Then, one night in the spring, the sister was alone in her room when she saw something move on the lawn outside her window.

"Gradually she became aware of two lights," Hare says in his earnest account, "which flickered in and out in the belt of trees which separated the lawn from an adjacent churchyard, and, as her gaze became fixed upon them, she saw them emerge, fixed in a dark substance, a definite ghastly something which seemed every moment to become nearer, increasing in size and substance as it approached. Every now and then it was lost for a moment in the long shadows which stretched across the lawn from the trees, and then it emerged larger than ever, and still coming on ..."

The woman, transfixed in horror, was unable to utter a cry as the hideous creature glided up to her window until a pane fell out, and then a bony hand reached in and lifted the latch.

"The window opened and the creature came in, and it came across the room, and the woman's terror was so great that she could not scream, and it came up to the bed, and it twisted its long, bony fingers into her hair, and it dragged her head over the side of the bed and—it bit her violently in the throat."

The woman then screamed. The creature fled into the night with the victim's two brothers in pursuit. One shot the creature in the leg. It was seen to dart into a burial vault on the Croglin Grange property.

The next day, the brothers summoned all the tenants of Croglin Grange and the vault was opened. All but one of the coffins within were in disarray. That one was intact, but its lid was slightly ajar. "They raised the lid and there—brown, withered, but quite entire—was the same hideous figure which had attacked the woman, with the marks of a recent pistol shot in the leg. They did the only thing that can lay a vampire—they burnt it."

How did the vampire myth get started? Raymond McNally thinks some historical accounts may be rooted in various obscure diseases.

"The disease porphyria seems to lurk behind vampire and werewolf stories from the past," he said. "This disorder usually causes deformation of the face, teeth, and nails. Another snydrome is extreme sensitivity to light, meaning porphyria victims in older times may have foraged for food at night because they could not physically endure the rays of the sun.

"Moreover, since porphyria, being hereditary, is a family disease its similarity to vampirism is all the more striking, for the vampire traditionally begins by attacking and thus infecting members of its own family."

Other stories of walking corpses may have arisen from cases of living burial, McNally suggests, in which victims of catalepsy, a deathlike coma, were mistakenly entombed. Still other cases may be based on bizarre forms of mental illness in which the victim suffered from the delusion that he was a vampire, a werewolf, a zombie, or whichever sort of monster was popular at the time.

But a deeper reason for the longevity of the vampire cult and its popularity in today's age of the computer is, suggests McNally, the nonrational side of human nature.

"There is a part of us," he says, "that wishes to believe that the impossible is possible. Daily life becomes so dull that one desires to escape into the unfamiliar, the unnatural, the unreal.

"At the same time, these vampire tales touch on something still deeper—our ignorance and fear of death, which is no less today than it was centuries ago."

82. The Ghost Hunting Clergyman

The reference is to Reverend Canon John Pearce-Higgins, recently retired vice-provost of London's Southwark Cathedral and Britain's foremost ecclesiastical ghost hunter.

He has also been called "a twentieth-century exorcist" (an exorcist being somebody who casts out evil spirits), but this, he says, is a bit of a misnomer. The "unpaying guests" he deals with are not evil, but merely confused, unhappy, or at worst stupid spirits. And he does not cast them out but rather invites them, nicely, to leave.

"Haunted houses," the canon told me in a recent interview, "are not inhabited by devils or demons but by discarnate human beings—in other words, dead people—who usually don't know they are dead. They are earthbound spirits who have got lost or stuck amid the surroundings of their former earthly life."

Canon Pearce-Higgins realizes that for many people the idea of ghosts takes some believing. And he admits, to be sure, that many alleged hauntings are simply cases of bad plumbing, bats in the attic, or hysteria.

"But when all the superstition, misobservation, or exaggeration has been discounted," he said, "there remains a body of solid evidence, from ancient and modern times, of apparitions, unaccountable movements of objects, knockings, weird cries, and other ghostly phenomena.

"In Britain, hardly a month passes without reports of a family terrified out of their wits by some strange happening."

If there are such things as earthbound spirits, "stuck" (as the canon puts it) amid their former surroundings, how does one go about getting them unstuck?

"I have found," said the ghost hunting cleric, "that the only satisfactory way is to go to the haunted house with a psychic medium and let the medium get in touch with whatever distressed spirit is there. Then I usually hold a service of holy communion, a requiem for the restless dead.

"In one case, for five years a family living in an ancient house had endured phantom footsteps, doors opening and shutting of their own accord, books being hurled about, moans and groans, and even terrifying wailing cries.

"The medium contacted a tragedy apparently dating from Tudor times. There were present the spirits of a number of monks, and a pitiful girl who said that she had had an illegitimate child who was killed, and that she herself was kept prisoner there and finally poisoned.

"Through the medium, in trance, I spoke with one of the monks, an evil character, who told me that the place was a priory. Not any more, I corrected him. My task was to convince the monks and the unhappy girl that they were dead and urge them to seek the light."

To help them on their way, the canon prayed, "O thou unquiet spirits, go thy way rejoicing that the prayers of the faithful shall follow thee and that thou mayest enjoy everlasting rest."

The disturbances ceased, Canon Pearce-Higgins said. And, interestingly, it turned out that indeed the place had been a priory until it was closed in 1536 when Henry VIII dissolved the English monasteries.

Once, in a case involving a haunted vicarage, the canon enlisted the aid of his ecclesiastical superior, the Right Reverend Mervyn Stockwood, Bishop of Southwark. The cause of the disturbances, said the ghost hunter, proved to be a former vicar who was guilt-ridden by past sins. When the unhappy wraith received absolution from the bishop, the disturbances promptly ceased.

Is the canon's de-ghosting procedure, as some would argue, merely a form of suggestion which works by quieting the emotions of those who live in the purportedly haunted house?

"Well of course," he said, "it is possible that the spirits we contact are products of our imagination, and that by being, as it were, dug out from the subconscious minds of those concerned, a release of emotional tension is achieved.

"However, I am inclined to believe that in most cases, really objective figures of deceased but earthbound persons are involved."

83. A Message From the Dead

One of the most vexed questions in the world of the unexplained is: Do the dead communicate?

Besides the fact that the question assumes the very thing to be proved—namely, that the dead are somehow in a position to communicate—it is a vexed one because fraud and fantasy abound.

There are plenty of phony spirit mediums who for a fee will guarantee to put you in touch with your dear departed Aunt Wilhemina. And there are, alas, only too many people only too willing to believe anything if they want to believe it.

However, there are some cases of alleged communication from the dead impressive enough to merit careful consideration. Such as this one.

The case is reported by the Reverend Theodore Tiemeyer, minister of Christ Congregational Church, Miami. It involved the late great American medium Arthur Ford. Here is Mr. Tiemeyer's account.

"When I was a student at Eden Theological Seminary I often attended the First Congregational Church of Webster Grove, Mo. The minister there sometimes lectured at the seminary.

"His name was Irvine E. Inglis, pronounced as though it were Ingles. The information I received about him in later years was that his first wife had died and he remarried. I didn't hear about his own death.

"In 1966, however, at a seance with the medium Arthur Ford, I got a message from his minister. Ford gave the name Inglis and pronounced it both ways. He added, 'This man says his first name was Peter.'

"I said that I knew a Dr. Inglis but not named Peter. Nevertheless, Ford insisted that was his name.

"He said that this minister had in his library a book by a Canadian whose name he couldn't recall but he thought was

Alfred. The important thing was that the dead man had marked something in that book—a poem that was very significant to him.

"The message concluded with greetings to the dead man's loved ones, especially his widow.

"Well, I didn't know if any of this was correct but I checked it out. I contacted Dr. Inglis' widow.

"She was very happy to hear from me because she said she had become very interested herself in possible communication with the dead. I asked her about the book by the Canadian author and she said she would look in her husband's library.

"There she found one book by a Canadian—a man named Albert, not Alfred, Cliffe. More important, she said, her husband had underlined a poem in that book and written under it the words, 'This is I.'

"That poem, incredibly, was about the disciple Peter!

"Later, Dr. Inglis' son told me it had been the custom of his father's intimate friends, and only them, to call him Peter."

The puzzling questions raised by Mr. Tiemeyer's account are two:

How did the medium, Arthur Ford, know that the dead man had in his library one book by a Canadian with a poem in it specially marked?

How did he know that the dead man's intimates, and apparently only they, called him Peter?

84. The Swimming Dead?

Stories of the walking dead we've all heard—but the *swimming* dead?

Well, on December 4, 1929, the oil tanker *S.S. Watertown*, owned by the Cities Service Company, was the scene of a burial at sea. Two crewmen, James T. Courtney and Michael Meehan, were suffocated by gasoline fumes while the ship was en route from San Pedro, California to the Panama Canal. Their bodies were consigned to water more than a thousand-feet deep off the west coast of Mexico.

It was the next day that the ship's first mate reported spotting the two men—the two *dead* men—in the water off the port rail. By the time the tanker reached the Panama Canal, virtually every crew member had seen the weird apparitions.

The likenesses, which witnesses agreed were definitely those of Courtney and Meehan, appeared daily in early evening. They were always about 40 feet from the ship, as though swimming steadily after it.

The ghostly heads disappeared as soon as the tanker left the Pacific and entered the canal. Before the return voyage, the ship's skipper, Captain Keith Tracy, bought a camera. If the heads reappeared he meant to photograph them.

And they did reappear. Once the *Watertown* was in the Pacific again the two apparitions were seen, swimming after the ship.

Capt. Tracy took six exposures, then locked the film in his cabin safe.

The film was developed in New York by a commercial photographer. Five of the shots showed nothing unusual but the sixth revealed two images—one hazy, the other clearly recognizable as Michael Meehan, bald head and all.

James S. Patton, an officer of the Cities Service Company, had the negative and print of the eerie photograph examined by experts at New York's Burns Detective Agency. No evidence of hanky-panky was found.

A crazy story?

Of course.

Unbelievable?

Well, maybe and maybe not.

Here's a fact: For some years an enlargement of the ghost picture was displayed in the offices of the Cities Service Co., at 70 Pine Street, New York.

There, thousands of people saw for themselves two men swimming in a heavy sea their heads riding the crest of the waves. One of the men had blurred features but showed a definite resemblance to James Courtney. The other man was easily recognizable to any who knew him as the dead seaman, Meehan.

Was the picture some sort of optical freak? A bizarre natural phenomenon? A hoax? An utterly wild coincidence? Or two ghosts.

That's part of the unexplained . . .

85. De-Ghosting a Haunted House

Getting rid of household pests is hardly a glamorous job. Unless, of course, the pest happens to be a ghost.

In the Middle Ages it was the custom when dealing with a haunted house to form a magic circle and, by the use of spells and enchantments, to "lay" the ghost—that is, put it out of business.

A modern version of this medieval ritual is the "rescue circle" which reportedly has been successful in de-ghosting a number of contemporary haunted houses. Danton Walker's, for instance.

The late Broadway columnist of the *New York Daily News* in 1942 bought a house in the Ramapo Mountains some 50 miles from Manhattan. The house, of pre-Revolutionary vintage, was reputed to be the scene of an unfriendly haunting.

Walker was a sophisticated man, not unduly prone to superstition. Yet from the start he sensed an air of subtle menace about the house, a great sadness. In his third year of occupancy strange manifestations began and gradually escalated into a full-blown haunting.

The symptoms were classic: Mysterious thumps and raps which got steadily louder as time went by; eerie moans and wails; phantom footsteps thudding up and down the hallways at night; unnatural icy drafts; and the lights flickering off and on.

The payoff came one night when a weekend guest awoke in a state of trauma at finding the blanket being whisked off his bed by unseen hands.

Danton Walker decided that either he or the ghost must go. But who does one consult about evicting such an uninvited guest?

On somebody's advice, Walker sought the help of Eileen Garrett, famous medium and at the time president of the eminently respectable Parapsychology Foundation in New York. Mrs. Garrett suggested a rescue circle to get rid of the ghost.

(It should be noted that though the rescue circle method

implies that the ghost is an actual spirit, this is not necessarily so. In fact, most parapsychologists probably subscribe to the view that a "ghost" is an impersonal bundle of violent psychic energy, the fallout from an emotional explosion which may have occurred centuries ago.)

On a cold, gray afternoon in November, 1952, the rescue circle drove out to Danton Walker's country home. Besides Mrs. Garrett and Walker, the group included New York psychiatrist Dr. Robert W. Laidlaw, a psychical researcher, and a secretary with a tape-recorder.

The group gathered in the upstairs bedroom which Danton Walker said had been the scene of the most violent manifestations. The time was 2:45. The room was filled with pale daylight.

In a brisk, businesslike way, the medium prepared to go into a trance. As she induced the auto-hypnotic state, her breathing became heavy and irregular, her face twitched slightly.

Suddenly her "control" Uvani, came through. (A "control" is the trance-personality which regularly manifests through a particular medium. Uvani claimed to have been an Arab who lived on earth a hundred years ago.)

Uvani announced that there was indeed a disturbing presence which he identified as a Revolutionary soldier who had been tortured by the British in that very room. The soldier's ordeal, said Uvani, had unhinged his mind and he did not realize that he was dead. He was "earthbound," trapped in a limbo between worlds.

The ghost's only hope for peace was to seek it in the beyond, said Uvani, and the task of the rescue circle was to persuade him of this.

Then Uvani announced that he was withdrawing to allow the ghost to speak through the medium.

The medium's face changed into a contorted mask. Madness stared from her eyes. When she spoke, the voice was broken, incoherent.

The ghost, through the medium, poured out a pitiful story of horror and confusion. At one point the medium fell to the floor with a howl of pain and writhed.

Dr. Laidlaw, the psychiatrist, spoke for the circle. In soothing, therapeutic tones, he comforted the ghost and urged him to depart that scene of bitter memories and find peace.

Finally the ghost, speaking through the medium, accepted that he was "dead" and agreed to leave the place. Thereupon

Mrs. Garrett crumpled like an empty sack. Presently, life seemed to return to her body. She stirred and sat up.

The time was four o'clock.

Danton Walker reported that from that time the house was untroubled.

Was the "ghost" a "place memory?"

In this theory, a haunting is not an actual visitation by a restless spirit but the playback of unhappy images from the past, like a rerun on television.

The rescue circle may succeed because it acts as a psychic catharsis which purges the place of its unhappy memories.

At any rate, satisfied customer Danton Walker allowed that it worked.

86. Abraham Lincoln Still in the White House?

Does the ghost of Abraham Lincoln still walk the halls of the White House?

This question came up in a conversation I had in Washington, D. C., with a senator who shares my interest in psychic phenomena.

The senator said that there have been those in recent years who reported seeing Mr. Lincoln prowling his old haunts, as it were.

Mrs. Eleanor Roosevelt, wife of F.D.R., was one of those who took such reports seriously. As a matter of fact, she had her own theory of what a haunting was and it agreed with the views held by many scientists who have studied the phenomenon.

Mrs. Roosevelt believed that, as she put it, any place where someone had lived hard would quite likely be haunted by that individual's personality.

Parapsychologists—scientists who study psychic phenomena—believe that a house can retain impressions of those who have lived in it, long after the occupants are dead. This is particularly true if the occupant had a powerful personality, and even more so if the dwelling was the scene of strong emotionalism or tragic events.

This theory may account for the numerous reported sightings of the ghost of Abraham Lincoln in the White House. Certainly he had a powerful personality. And certainly he experienced tragedy, as well as triumph, in the executive mansion.

Mrs. Eleanor Roosevelt told the following story:

"I was sitting in my study downstairs when one of the maids burst in on me in a state of great excitement. I looked up from my work and asked her what the trouble was."

" 'He's up there—sitting on the edge of the bed and taking off his shoes' she exclaimed. 'Who's up there taking off his shoes?' I asked. 'Mr. Lincoln, Mr. Lincoln,' the maid replied."

Mrs. Roosevelt said she had always felt that Lincoln's bedroom was haunted by what she called a serene and dignified presence.

One more example of the unexplained!

87. The Ghost Picked a Winning Number

The story of a ghost who picked a winning number is just about the farthest-out of all the far-out tales I've investigated.

But it is attested by the sworn statements of the man to whom it happened, a bank security guard in Philadelphia, and his two brothers who were witnesses.

The man is Clement Tamburrino and the "ghost" was Fletcher, the so-called spirit guide of famed medium Arthur Ford (who convinced the late Bishop James Pike that he had contacted his dead son). When Ford put himself into a trance, Fletcher, claiming to be a French-Canadian who died in 1918, spoke through him.

Clem Tamburrino, a close friend of Ford until the medium's death in 1971, recounts his astounding experience with Fletcher in my biography, *Arthur Ford: The Man Who Talked With the Dead.* Here is how Tamburrino tells it.

"Fletcher said to me one day, 'You have no money.' And I said, 'No, I haven't. I haven't worked for a while because of a bad back.'

"And Fletcher said, 'Well, I'm going to give you a number to play.' I was taken aback. I don't play the numbers game. I never bet on a horse race in my life. I don't gamble. It just isn't my thing.

"But Fletcher gave me a number and told me to play it in the numbers game the following Saturday. It was 217. And he said, 'Bankroll it heavily.'

"I decided to put fifteen dollars on the number. My brother, who didn't know about Fletcher's advice, said I was out of my mind. Most people play a dollar or two on the numbers. Some five. Some crazy ones ten. And here I was putting down fifteen and I don't have any money!

"So it was Saturday afternoon and I went upstairs to take a nap. And the number writer calls and says to my brother, 'You have the first number.'

"My brother Sam tells my other brother Frank and they agree that things are looking a little better. Maybe I'll have beginner's luck.

"About an hour later the number writer calls again and tells Sam, 'You have the second number.' So Sam's excited and he rushes to tell me, and I said, 'Call me when the third one comes.'

"Well, at five o'clock, or 5:30, the number writer calls and says I've won.

"Now, my brothers want to know how I did it. They knew I was going up to see Arthur Ford and that he was supposed to talk to a spook. So I told them how I got the number."

Tamburrino's winnings were substantial, he said. Later, when he tried to express tangibly his appreciation by offering to buy Arthur Ford a new coat, Fletcher sniffed: "Ford doesn't need a new coat."

Then the "ghost" with the winning touch added tartly: "Besides, Ford didn't give you that number. I did."

88. The Photograph and the Dead Man

If a person's name appears in a newspaper mistakenly under somebody else's photograph, the person is bound to be annoyed.

But what if he's dead?

In 1970, in Bradenton, Florida, reporter Sally Remaley

wrote a story on the local post office for the Bradenton *Herald*. The story featured a photograph of the town's first postmaster, Major William Iridell Turner. However, by mistake somebody else's picture was used above Major Turner's name.

After the story appeared, Sally Remaley received a phone call from Mrs. Gladys Pitman, granddaughter of Bradenton's first postmaster. Mrs. Pitman said that apparently her dead grandfather was annoyed when the other man's picture appeared above his name.

On the day the story ran, reported Mrs. Pitman, a photograph of the real Maj. Turner, which had hung for many years on the wall in her home, suddenly crashed to the floor. Curious, Sally Remaley asked Mrs. Pitman the exact time the picture had fallen and the latter was able to tell her.

Checking, the reporter was interested to discover that at that very time the wrong photographic engraving was being processed in the newspaper's composing room. The strange fall of the picture had coincided with the positioning of the wrong engraving in the page of type.

Mrs. Pitman said she believed her grandfather had "spoken up" to express his exasperation over the mistake. She pointed out that the picture had hung securely on the wall through several hurricanes. Moreover, the glass on the picture didn't break in the fall, which was surprising, and the nail didn't come out of the wall.

In fact, said Mrs. Pitman, the nail, when she checked, was tilting upwards, suggesting that the picture had "jumped" off it.

Of course, every rational person knows that inanimate objects don't jump off walls. If it jumped it must have had helped. But from what source?

The idea that a dead man could have anything to do with the strange behavior of his photograph is crazy. But then, many crazy things happen in this puzzling world.

What we have here is another case of the strange pairing of events which seemed related and yet cannot be—at least, in any sense that science can understand.

The link between a mistake and a dead man's photograph falling to the floor, without the nail being loose and without any damage to the picture, glass or frame, is part of the unexplained.

89. A Ghost for the Defense

Many sober witnesses have reported seeing a ghost. But not many ghosts can have been cited in court as part of the defense of an accused man. At least one was, however.

It happened in London in the summer of 1966. Twenty-year-old William Haywood, a married man, appeared in a magistrate's court on charges arising from four incidents of alleged reckless driving.

Haywood's attorney asked the court for a fine instead of a possible jail sentence on the grounds that his client had been under peculiar emotional stress.

"The cause of the stress," explained the attorney, "is a ghost."

A ghost? One imagines that at this the magistrate who no doubt thought he had heard everything, perked up.

"The house my client lives in," the attorney told the court, "is haunted. A local minister has attempted to lay the ghost. My client's wife is terrified of seeing the ghost and of being in the house by herself. She also is expecting a baby."

Valerie Haywood, the accused's wife, testified that she had seen the ghost several times.

"He's an old man," she informed the court. "He's dressed in black Victorian clothes. And he has a gold stud at his collar."

The ghost, she added, "appears in a bedroom at seven or eight o'clock at night. He has gray hair. He just stands there in the middle of the room.

"He doesn't look evil but he terrifies me. Even our spaniel Lassie won't go into that room. She whimpers when she passes the door.

"I'm not normally a superstitious person but I'm having to be treated for nerves since we've lived in this house.

"We were warned by the people who have lived there before, not to take the place but we laughed at them.

"We were told that a man went insane in that bedroom many years ago and it's his ghost that haunts it."

William Haywood supported his wife's account.

"I've seen the ghost too," he testified. "I call him the man in black. We don't use that bedroom now."

After hearing the story of the Haywood's unpaying guest the court let the accused off with a fine because of what the magistrate called "the special circumstances."

90. Royalty and the Spirits

Among my recently completed projects was a biography of the late Arthur Ford, the medium whom Bishop James Pike said had enabled him to communicate with his dead son. (That was during a seance televised in September, 1967, which I arranged and moderated.)

One of the colorful parts of Ford's story was the many seances he conducted for royalty. He gave a "sitting" as it's called, in 1928 to Sweden's Queen Maud which so impressed her that she bestowed on Ford a diamond-studded signet that he later gave to his wife as a wedding present.

One of my favorite anecdotes about Arthur Ford was when, a couple of nights before the Pike television seance, my wife and I went to the Park Plaza Hotel in Toronto, where Ford was staying, to take him to dinner.

Coming out of the hotel as we arrived was the entourage of King Constantine of Greece and his queen, who were on an official visit to Toronto.

When we met Arthur Ford, I said to him jokingly: "We should have invited the king to a seance."

"Yes," he agreed, lighting a cigar, "I knew his uncle very well."

Ford wasn't kidding. King George II of Greece, Constantine's uncle, was a constant attender of seances during the decade he spent in exile in London until the 1935 restoration of the Greek monarchy. Constantine's father, King Paul, was also deeply interested in seances and made no attempt to hide the fact.

As a matter of fact, European royalty always has had a curious affinity for the pyschic world.

The British royal family has a history of fascination with the occult going back at least to Queen Victoria. Her gillie, or manservant, John Brown, was reputed to have been a medium and the hours which Victoria and he spent closeted together, which occasioned some scandal at the time, are said to have been spent in trying to communicate with the old queen's much missed consort, Prince Albert.

In more recent times, the late Princess Marina, Duchess of Kent, was known as an avid psychic enthusiast. She invited a society clairvoyante, Nell St. John Montague, to her wedding.

London medium Lillian Bailey, whom I know, has as one of her most prized possessions a chair which once belonged to King George VI, father of the present queen.

The chair was given by the king to the speech therapist who helped him overcome his stammer—Lionel Logue, a convinced spiritualist. Logue then bequeathed the chair to the medium, Mrs. Bailey, in gratitude for seances he had attended with her.

No one knows whether the present queen has attended seances. However, the Queen Mother, widow of George VI, is reputed to be deeply interested. Indeed, she is said to have had a sort of private clairvoyant in the person of Tom Corbett. Corbett, whom I've met, is a charming elf with Irish charm and a crystal ball.

In 1958, the *London Sunday Pictorial* caused a sensation when it revealed that Corbett had given sittings to the Queen Mother at Clarence House. The clairvoyant and the newspaper stuck by their story for 48 hours in the face of official denials from Buckingham Palace. The newspaper published a photograph of Corbett entering the gates to the Queen Mother's residence.

However, protocol prevailed and Tom Corbett officially said that reports he had been consulted by the Queen Mother were untrue. However, people who know him say the denial was untrue and was made only to avoid offending royal sensibilities to unwelcome publicity.

91. The Possession of Lucy Vennum

Most stories of alleged "possession"—the control of a living person's body by a spirit—are "nut stuff". But is this true of all such stories?

A few contemporary psychiatrists—for example, Dr. Ian Stevenson of the University of Virginia medical school and Dr. Robert Laidlaw, formerly of New York's Roosevelt Hospital—have said that they take seriously the possibility of possession. And one purported case, that of Lucy Vennum, was inexplicable enough to impress a thinker of the stature of William James, the greatest of American psychologists.

In his standard text, *The Principles of Psychology*, James recounted this eerie story of a schoolgirl apparently possessed by someone who had been dead for more than a decade.

The story began in February, 1878, in the town of Watseka, Illinois. A 14-year-old girl named Lurancy—"Lucy" to her parents and friends—Vennum suffered a series of strange, trancelike seizures. During one of these "fits," as her family called them, the girl underwent an incredible transformation.

She awoke from the seizure a different person. At least, to all intents and purposes she was a different person. She professed not to recognize her parents and demanded to know who they were and where she was. Most curious of all, she said her name was not Lucy Vennum but Mary Roff, and she insisted on being taken to her home.

A young woman named Mary Roff, aged 19, had died in the same town 12 years before.

The physician on the case, Dr. W.E. Stevens (who later wrote a full account of the phenomenon) appears to have assumed, not unnaturally, that he was dealing with a bizarre form of insanity. With love and understanding it might pass, he advised Lucy's parents, but in the meantime humor the girl so far as possible.

The personality calling herself Mary Roff refused to stay in the Vennum household. The family of the deceased Miss

Roff, apprised of the strange situation, were sympathetic. They said that Lucy could stay with them, if it would help, until her bizarre delusion passed.

What happened then sounds so fantastic, even impossible, that one is tempted to dismiss the account as sheer fiction. However, both William James, as I've said, and Richard Hodgson, a psychical researcher noted for his skeptical caution, were convinced that the account was substantially true.

For three months an unearthly drama unfolded in the Roff household. The Mary personality astounded the Roffs with her detailed knowledge of each member of the family, and of the deceased Miss Roff's personal possessions, the house, and other matters with which the dead girl properly would have been familiar.

Once Mrs. Roff said to the Mary personality: "Do you remember when the stove pipe fell down and your brother, Frank, was burned?"

"Of course," replied the girl, and she indicated the very spot on the arm where Frank Roff had been burned.

On another occasion a sister asked the Mary personality if she remembered the old family dog.

"Yes," was the reply, and the girl promptly went outside and, pointing to a spot, said: "He died just there."

She was correct.

The Mary personality, according to the Roffs, always recognized friends of the deceased girl and, despite several attempts to trick her, never claimed to recognize anyone who had not been known to Mary Roff.

The incredible interlude came to an end on May 21, 1878, when, after giving a few days' notice, the Mary Roff personality relinquished control of the body. Following a brief period of cataleptic sleep, Lucy Vennum awoke as her old self. She greeted the Roffs cooly and asked to be taken home.

So far as is known, Lucy suffered no recurrence of her bizarre identity switch.

What can we say about this curious story?

Was it an example of multiple personality, as described in the book—*The Three Faces of Eve*? In that celebrated case a woman's personality, under the shock of emotional trauma, split into two, then three, distinct selves. This had nothing to do with spirit possession. The three personalities ultimately we've blended into one by psychiatric treatment.

However, in the case of Lucy Vennum how could the

Mary Roff personality have known intimate details of the dead girl's life? By ESP?

Or is it even remotely conceivable that for three months a girl was indeed possessed by a dead woman?

92. The Ghost of an Event

Can a place be haunted by the ghost not of a person but of an event?

There is some curious evidence that events, particularly those charged with strong emotion, can leave an imprint behind.

Perhaps you could say that an emotional explosion releases fallout which lingers long after the original event is past.

"It is," said my friend, the late Dr. Nandor Fodor, a distinguished psychoanalyst, "as if a house or some other place had a memory of its own.

Somehow memory seems to be an exudation from the place, permeating everything on the spot."

Here is a true story, told to me by Mrs. Lucille Kahn of New York, which suggests that events do indeed leave ghosts behind.

One evening, at the home of Mr. and Mrs. David Kahn on East 80th Street in New York, several guests were enjoying a dinner party. The guests included an Episcopal bishop, a priest, and an editor of a large publishing house.

After dinner the conversation turned to extrasensory perception, a subject in which everyone present was deeply interested.

Suddenly, the editor, who was diabetic, began to shake violently. He had time to gasp out that he was going into insulin shock—a reaction from having taken too much of the drug which controls diabetes—and then slumped to the floor.

His body writhed, his arms and legs flailing, while a stream of profanity poured from his lips of a man normally gentle, shy, and cultivated.

Lucille Kahn rushed to the kitchen for a glass of orange juice to counteract the excess insulin in the editor's bloodstream. When she returned the seizure was over. The editor, trembling, pale, and mortified, gratefully took the orange juice and excused himself.

Though he later rejoined the dinner party the editor was abnormally subdued. His frightening seizure had cast a shadow over the evening.

About a year after this incident the noted medium, Arthur Ford, visited Mr. and Mrs. Kahn. He sat in the same chair which had been occupied by the editor. As Ford and his hosts were chatting before dinner an extraordinary thing happened.

Ford appeared to be vaguely uncomfortable, then in real distress. As the Kahns watched, incredulously, the medium appeared to reenact the unhappy incident which had taken place a year before.

He complained of feeling terribly ill, his body trembled and then twitched uncontrollably, and finally he crumpled to the floor, his arms and legs jerking.

In those moments Ford reproduced almost exactly the behavior of the editor during his insulin shock—an incident of which the medium apparently could not have known.

But Ford's seizure was not due to insulin for he didn't take the drug. What, then, had caused it?

Ford himself said to the Kahns: "What happened in this room? Something happened here which I unconsciously tuned into."

Then, the Kahns told him of the incident a year before which they had seen eerily before their eyes.

93. The Man Who Wasn't There

The strange and unexpected can happen to anybody, any time. It did—to a pair of suburban housewives.

This story is true. I know the people to whom it happened. Their identities are not disclosed for personal reasons.

It was August 1, 1972, between 3:30 and 4 P.M. Two housewives, neighbors in a suburb of Toronto, were chatting on the back patio of one of their homes. The day was sunny.

Suddenly one of the women said: "There's Dick"—Dick being her husband. She pointed to the next backyard, the backyard of her home. Her neighbor looked and she, too saw Dick.

Dick, a clergyman, had on a pair of white shorts that he often wore around the house in the summer, and no shirt. The neighbor remarked on his good tan and, idly, asked wife why she didn't buy him a pair of colored shorts for a change.

Dick was visible to both women for about five minutes. Then they saw him turn and walk back toward the house, disappearing behind a hillside.

Now comes the eerie part of the story. It appears that Dick was *not* in the yard when the two women saw him there.

When Dick's wife entered their house about 20 minutes later, she was surprised to find him stretched out on the bed asleep. He still had on a blue sports shirt and blue trousers that he had worn the previous night during an all-night drive from Philadelphia.

When his wife awakened him, Dick insisted that he had not been in the yard. And as for wearing his white shorts— where were they? He said he didn't even know that.

Dick has only two pairs of white shorts. The women agreed that the pair he was wearing when they saw him had an elasticized back. That particular pair turned out to be at the bottom of a laundry basket, jammed under dirty sheets and blankets. Dick's wife said she remembered putting them there more than a week earlier. The second pair of white shorts was still unpacked in Dick's suitcase; he had taken them on his vacation but hadn't worn them. They were smooth and uncreased.

What happened?

Well, there are several possibilities.

The first, which will occur to any ordinary skeptical person, is that the whole incident is a practical joke. However Dick and his wife and their neighbor insist it wasn't a joke.

The second theory is mistaken identity. But the only man in the neighborhood who remotely resembled Dick was out of town for the day. Besides, the two women insisted they could not have been mistaken.

Another possibility is that Dick walked in his sleep, undressed, donned his white shorts (after digging them out of the laundry basket), went outside, came back in, doffed the shorts, redressed himself, and got back into bed—all without being aware of what he was doing.

Arguing against this theory is the fact that Dick, so far as he or his wife knows, has never walked or ever talked in his sleep. (A psychonalyst told me that the odds were strongly against a person with no history of somnambulism suddenly becoming a full-blown sleepwalker.)

A fourth possibility is that the incident was a shared hallucination. In other words, Dick's wife and the neighbor (who is married to a doctor) projected the figure out of their minds, in the same way that a hypnotized person can be made to see a pink elephant or anything else.

The only trouble with this theory, said a psychiatrist I consulted, is that collective hallucinations (involving two or more persons) are "exceedingly rare," though apparently they do happen.

If it were a double hallucination, however, what triggered it? Why should both women suddenly see, and watch, for a full five minutes, the same hallucinated figure?

Still another possibility is so-called psychic projection. The theory is that human beings possess two bodies—the physical form we're all familiar with and a second body known as the "psychic double."

Under certain circumstances, this second body is said to be able to separate temporarily from the physical and travel about on its own. Interestingly, such psychic projections are alleged to occur most often when the person is in a trance, coma, or deep sleep.

Dick, of course, recovering from an exhausting all-night drive, was asleep when the two women saw whomever or whatever they saw.

94. The Poltergeist Psychoanalyzed

"So-called ghosts are perfectly real," said Dr. Hans Bender, "and properly understood, perfectly natural."

Dr. Bender, a noted ghost-hunter, was chatting with me in his office at West Germany's Freiburg University where he is a professor and director of the Institute for Border Areas of Psychology.

The 66-year-old physician has spent more than two decades pursuing the elusive poltergeist.

The German word "poltergeist" (meaning literally, "noisy spirit") describes those mysterious outbreaks, usually in a house, when dishes start smashing themselves against the wall, bottles pop their corks and light bulbs explode, bangs and thumps resound all over the place, and other bizarre things go on.

In some cases a flesh-and-blood prankster is responsible but in others the prankster is invisible—a poltergeist. In such genuine cases, says Dr. Bender, the cause is "psychokinesis" or "PK" for short—that is, psychic energy unconsciously released by the focal person which acts directly on physical objects.

"I've investigated 38 poltergeist cases," Dr. Bender said, "and believe me, they defy normal scientific explanation."

Take one of the most spectacular and best documented cases, which occurred in the fall of 1967 in the town of Rosenheim, 40 miles from Munich.

In the office of lawyers Siegfried Adam it was suddenly hellzapoppin. Light bulbs exploded with enough force to bury splinters of glass in the wall. Neon tubes unscrewed themselves from their sockets. Hanging light fixtures swung wildly back and forth with no visible means of propulsion. And the telephones went crazy—the law office was billed for hundreds of calls which the staff denied having made.

To solve the mystery the local electric company installed instruments to monitor all electrical equipment in the office, and the telephone company put in a device which automatically recorded all outgoing calls.

The result was an even deeper mystery. Though the electric company's instruments registered "tremendous deflections" which indicated some serious malfunction in the electrical system this malfunction was never traced.

The telephone company recorded no fewer than 60 calls in a single hour which the office employees insisted they had not made. Even more curious, all these were to the same number, one which provided callers with the correct time.

The chief of the electric company's maintenance company admitted on television: "Our experts cannot explain these extraordinary occurrences. It is all very strange."

The telephone company, for its part, kept insisting that somebody must be placing those outgoing calls—at a steady rate of one per minute—though the culprit was never caught.

However, who but a peculiarly crazy prankster would

phone for the correct time every minute, day after day for weeks?

When Dr. Bender arrived on the scene at the first of December the strange doings were still in full swing and driving everybody mad.

After calling in physicists, who conducted their own tests and confirmed that "some unknown form of energy is at work," Dr. Bender offered his diagnosis: A poltergeist.

The disturbances, he noted, never occurred on weekends but only when the staff were in the office. By a process of careful checking he zeroed in on the primary suspect—a 19-year-old unmarried secretary named Annemarie Schaberl.

Talking with her, Dr. Bender found that she was very unhappy, feeling hemmed in by an overly strict father and a job she didn't like.

"She was," said Dr. Bender, "a typical poltergeist.

"You see, these disturbances come from an actual emotional disorder. These people are usually young, often adolescents, with very intense conflicts, especially sexual ones, and a very low tolerance of frustration.

"What happens is that quite unconsciously—they are not aware of it at all—the emotional conflict is converted into PK which causes the phenomena."

Dr. Bender interpreted the hundreds of phone calls for the correct time as being due to Annemarie's feeling that the work day would never end.

"When you're frustrated you may throw a cup at the wall. In a poltergeist case the same sort of thing happens but by PK. The motivation however, is exactly the same."

The disturbances ceased when Annemarie happily married, said Dr. Bender.

He added a humorous postscript.

"Annemarie was engaged to another man before she met her husband. He was a bowling fan who used to take her to bowling alleys equipped with an electrical apparatus that set up the pins. When Annemarie was around, this apparatus usually refused to work.

"Finally, her fiancé dropped her, saying how could he marry a girl who did funny things to electrical gadgets.

"My own interpretation is that Annemarie unconsciously knew he wasn't the right man for her and used her PK to discourage him."

95. The Exorcist in Real Life

With demonomania sweeping the country in the wake of the movie *The Exorcist*, many intelligent people are asking: Could it be for real? Do such things actually happen?

The movie (in the unlikely event you don't already know) depicts the mysterious and terrifying experiences of a 12-year-old girl possessed by the devil. The author of the novel and the screenplay, William Peter Blatty, claims the story is based on fact.

From the standpoint of parapsychology—the scientific study of psychic phenomena—the trouble with *The Exorcist* is that it mixes a drop of fact with a gallon of fiction.

To understand the difference between science and superstition, consider a real case of purported evil possession that occurred in October, 1970, in the Ontario city of St. Catharines.

The haunted individual (called by parapsychologists the "focal person") was, as in *The Exorcist*, a youngster at the age of puberty—11-year-old Peter Walchuk. He lived with his parents in a modest apartment behind a store.

The strange noises came first. They were eerie scratchings, then raps and thumps, coming, it seemed, from inside the walls of the apartment.

Next, furniture began moving, apparently under its own power, and doors opened and closed by themselves. Then holes appeared in the plaster walls of boy's bedroom as though punched out by an invisible hammer.

The city engineering department was called to check if structural changes in the building could account for the queer goings-on.

"We satisfied ourselves there were no such problems," said Mel Holenski, St. Catherines' assistant city engineer.

On February 2, 1970 men from the gas company checked the furnace in the building and found it working normally.

A number of police officers summoned by the distraught parents reported witnessing inexplicable phenomena. One policeman told reporter Ron Whitmarsh of the St. Catharines

Standard that, while he watched, a large chair rose from the floor with the boy sitting on it, then tipped backwards pinning him against the wall.

The chair, the officer added, was "much too heavy" for the boy to have moved himself.

Things got spookier. More than one policeman reported seeing the boy's bed shake violently and then rise straight up almost to the ceiling.

Several lawyers representing the owner of the building witnessed the eerie events. One saw a footstool on which the boy was sitting fly from under him as though yanked by unseen hands.

A lawyer who visited the haunted apartment left his overcoat there and was reported too scared to return for it.

The family was Roman Catholic and two priests were summoned. They kept their lips sealed about what they had seen but evidently were impressed because on February 16, 1970, the Catholic bishop of St. Catharines, Thomas J. McCarthy, told a reporter he believed "something supernatural" was preying on the boy.

It was noted that the phenomena definitely centered on the boy. When he left the apartment for a few days to stay with relatives, the strange happenings subsided. When he returned, they started again.

The outcome of the mysterious affair?

Well, parapsychologists know from the study of numerous cases that such a "poltergeist outbreak," as it's called, usually burns itself out in a few days or at the most weeks. That's what happened. Within a month, the phenomena ended and everybody lived unhaunted ever after.

What caused the mysterious sounds and movements? Was it a devil, or a ghost? Or something projected from the boy's own mind?

Parapsychologists accept the latter view. In this interpretation a poltergeist outbreak is due not to some disembodied entity—whether spirit or demon, depending on your bias—but to emotional conflicts, possibly sex-related, within the unconscious mind of the focal young person. These conflicts unleash raw psychic energy—the same force that some people reportedly can use consciously to move small objects in the lab—and it is this that shifts furniture and produces unearthly noises.

A poltergeist haunting is a case of psychic measles. When the troubled youngster feels better, the haunting stops.

There are significant differences between this authentic case and the fictional story of *The Exorcist*.

In the movie the affected girl got that way, it's suggested, by playing with a ouija board; it's also pretty clearly implied that the fact her mother is irreligious may have had something to do with it.

In the actual case, the family was devoutly religious and the boy was more likely to be saying the rosary than fiddling with a ouija board.

In the movie, the evil spirit is only routed after a horrendous exorcism ritual in which one priest dies of heart failure and another leaps to his death.

In the actual case, no exorcism was performed and the household soon returned to normal.

96. Carry On Composing, Beethoven

Recently I paid a return visit in London to the world's most remarkable composer—Mrs. Rosemary Brown.

This middle-aged widow is remarkable for two reasons.

First, in spite of virtually no musical training she has produced some 600 compositions in the exact styles of such celebrated composers as Liszt, Beethoven, Chopin, Bach, Schubert, Brahms, and Rachmaninoff. The music is good enough to have won praise from some of Britain's leading musical figures and one of her string quartets in the style of Brahms recently was performed on the British Broadcasting Corporation.

Second, and even more unusual, is the fact that Mrs. Brown insists she is not a musical prodigy, a late-blooming genius who after years of working at such jobs as a dish washer in a school kitchen suddenly burst into creativity.

Rosemary Brown maintains that she is merely a stenographer. The music, she says, comes from a procession of dead composers.

As she tells the story, the whole strange business started in 1964 when Liszt appeared to her in a vision and said that he and some other deceased composers were going to communicate original music through her to convince the world that life after death is a fact.

How did they go about conveying their compositions to somebody who, in the opinion of British musicologist Mary Firth, "lacks even a basic musical ability"?

"Well," Mrs. Brown told me, "the fact that I knew practically nothing about music was an advantage because then, you see, people couldn't say the compositions were mine. But it did make things a bit difficult.

"Liszt began by simply guiding my hands at the piano. I almost felt as if somebody was putting my hands on like gloves and then playing through them.

"I didn't understand what the music was, I wouldn't even know what key it was in. I used to learn through the pattern of the notes on the keyboard. I simply knew whereabouts I'd got to put my hands next."

The next stage was when the composers switched to dictating the music, says Rosemary, giving her the key, the timing, the left hand, the right hand.

Today, Mrs. Brown has to her credit—or, as she insists, the dead composers have to theirs—piano sonatas, preludes, string quartets, and the first part of what she says is Beethoven's 10th Symphony.

"It's a choral symphony," she informed me matter-of-factly, "and it's magnificent. It will take me two or three years to get it down on paper."

According to Rosemary, Beethoven is not an easy taskmaster. If a dictation session is interrupted he's apt to burst out with "Mein Gott!" Generally, she says, he converses with her in English, which apparently he's picked up on the other side.

Rosemary Brown's story is crazy, of course. But look at her undeniable achievements:

Her music has been performed by leading concert artists such as Richard Rodney Bennett, Peter Katin, Louis Kentner, and Hepzibah Menuhin.

Phillips has issued a commercial record of her pieces called *A Musical Seance.*

The British firm of Novello is planning to publish a wide selection of her music.

Britain's leading Liszt expert, Humphrey Searle, examined a piece called "Grubelei" which Rosemary said had come from Liszt. Searle praised the composition, noted its uncanny resemblance to the great man's style, and concluded:

"This is the sort of piece which Liszt could well have

written, particularly during the last 15 years of his life when he was experimenting in new directions."

There are skeptics, of course, who insist that Mrs. Brown must be some kind of fake, but they are not sure just what kind. Is she a gigantic musical talent in her own right who for some weird reason is hiding it? Or is she being used by some mad genius lurking in the background?

To talk with Rosemary Brown over a cup of tea, as I have, is to be convinced of her total sincerity. Whether her extraordinary music reflects, as she says, contact from the dead or the hitherto untapped potential of her own creative self is a moot point.

However, Stewart Robb, a New Yorker who has a degree in concert Piano from London's Royal Academy of Music, says of Mrs. Brown:

"I believe her music comes from where she says it comes from—Beethoven, Liszt, Chopin, Schubert, and the rest. So far as I'm concerned, there's no other explanation."

97. Making A Ghost

Can you make a ghost?

Yes, it sounds nutty. But a group of sane, normal people in Toronto, under the supervision of a distinguished scientist, set out to try to do just that—make a ghost.

They've gotten some remarkable results.

It started in September 1972 when several members of the Toronto Society for Psychical Research were discussing whether a ghost or apparition is something conjured up by the mind of the beholder. If that's so, they speculated, why couldn't a ghost be deliberately conjured up?

There and then, eight persons agreed to meet once a week to spend an hour, possibly more, conjuring up a wholly imaginary ghost they named "Philip."

Before they were through, this mythical phantom was communicating with them in a variety of eerie ways.

If you're going to invent a ghost you might as well make him colorful and Philip was invested by his creators with a romantic aura. They made him an aristocratic Englishman who lived in the mid-1600s, had a beautiful but frigid wife whom he detested, and carried on a mad love affair with a raven-haired gypsy named Margo. When Margo was burned as a witch, Philip, heart-broken, hurled himself from the parapet of his castle.

The experiment in ghost-making was monitored by Dr. George Owen, formerly professor of genetics at Cambridge University, now of Toronto, a noted investigator of psychic phenomena. His wife Iris was a member of the group.

At first the ghost-makers tried to conjure up Philip by meditating, but nothing much happened. They switched to holding old-fashioned seances with everybody sitting around a table, singing loudly to "raise the power," and exhorting their made-up ghost to do something, anything, c'mon Philips, please.

He did!

It started with some funny raps from the table. These were too faint to be heard but were felt as slight pulsations. Soon they grew loud enough to be audible not only to the group but to others, such as Dr. Owen and a psychiatrist who attended some of the sessions. Both these witnesses said they had no doubt that the raps were genuinely "psychic."

Philip answered questions by rapping once for yes and twice for no. Sometimes, for variety, he caused raps to come from the wall or ceiling of the seance room.

Soon it was a custom for everybody at a seance to say goodnight to Philip and get an individual response—a rap that seemed to come from the table precisely under the person's extended hand. (The group used an ordinary plastic-topped, metal-legged card table.) I myself had this peculiar experience at a Philip seance.

The raps were just for starters. Before long the table came alive under Philip's influence and performed dramatic antics.

With some of the group always maintaining at least light finger contact with it. The table rocked in rhythm to music, bucked like a bronco, balanced on one leg, flipped completely over so that all four legs pointed straight up, and sometimes whooshed around so fast that the group found themselves scrambling to keep up.

Philip, for so young a ghost, proved to be not in the least bashful. He performed willingly for skeptics and for a television filming crew. (The film of Philip's feats is available.)

Comes the jackpot question: Has the mythical ghost

succeeded in getting all four legs of the table off the floor at the same time?

The answer from one of the group, Iris Owen, was a very tentative yes.

Tentative because though on one occasion the table was airborne, she says, it was to a height of only a fraction of an inch. The group wants to get the table floating unequivocally in mid-air. And they appear to be confident they can do it. Or at least, that Philip can.

"You have to believe implicitly that it's going to happen," explained Mrs. Owen, "before it does happen."

Dr. George Owen, an authority on ghosts, considers that the experiment's results have "remarkable implications." They show, he says, that "psychokinesis by committee" is possible (psychokinesis is the technical term for mind over matter).

If one group can make a ghost, Dr. Owen said, others can. None of the original group, he notes, claimed to have any special psychic gifts.

One of the ghost-makers, in the journal *New Horizons*, summed up their unique on-going experiment: "We've shown that in some manner we don't understand a group of people can create a thought-directed force which can be expressed in a physical way."

98. The Weeping Photograph

If the Rev. Robert Lewis' grandmother had been alive when he was ordained to the Epicopal priesthood, no doubt she would have wept for joy. She died, however, two years before the ordination.

Yet Canon Lewis wonders if his grandmother, in a curious way, did not after all weep at his ordination.

Canon Lewis is rector of St. Mary's Episcopal Church, Haddon Heights, New Jersey. His grandmother, who lived near Scranton, Pennsylvania, was Welsh-born and a very devout Baptist.

"My grandmother raised me pretty much," said Canon Lewis, "and always thought that I was the image of her husband, my grandfather, who died three years before I was born."

The priest's grandmother was a deeply religious, highly emotional person who, like many women, generally expressed great happiness by weeping. Whenever her grandson did something she especially proud of she wept for joy.

When Bob Lewis decided to become a priest and entered the Episcopal Divinity School in Philadelphia, his grandmother was overjoyed and, as usual, wept.

Sadly, she died of a brain hemorrhage two years before he completed his studies and was ordained.

But she may not have missed his ordination after all. This is how Canon Lewis himself finishes the story.

"In my room at the seminary I had a picture of my grandmother sitting on a chest of drawers.

"During my senior year of study I had to take my canonical exams before the bishop and his examining chaplain. This is both a written and oral test. If I passed it, I would be ordained. So it was a very important test indeed for me.

"It was at the end of April when I took the canonical exams and after the test the bishop informed me that I passed. On the way back to the seminary I had an emotional time thinking how happy and proud my grandmother would have been, knowing that I was to be ordained. But she had been dead for two years.

"When I got back to the seminary I went to my room and glanced at my grandmother's picture. To my astonishment it was soaking wet. Moisture had streaked my grandmother's face.

"The picture inside the glass of the frame was wet—so wet that the back of the picture was starting to buckle. There was a small pool of water under the picture where it had run onto the chest of drawers.

"Several seminarians came into my room and saw the wet photo and so did one of my professors. No one had an explanation," said Canon Lewis.

Examination of the photograph showed that the water seemed to have originated at the level of the eyes. Even after it dried, the picture showed streaks indicating that the water had streamed downward from the eyes.

"I felt," concluded Canon Lewis, "that my grandmother knew about my exams and that she had reacted in the way most typical of her—she cried."

If this photograph indeed showed human emotion, rather

than the incident being merely some bizarre coincidence (which of course is always possible), what sort of process could have been operating?

Dr. Nandor Fodor, a noted psychoanalyst and psychical researcher, investigated several cases of purported weeping statues and paintings, and decided that some were genuinely puzzling. He proposed the hypothesis of "at-oneness."

This, as Fodor conceived it, was the exact opposite of the psychological mechanism known as "identification," which is when a person feels such an intense emotional rapport with another individual, or thing, that he takes on the characteristics of that individual or thing. Thus, the devout person who develops the stigmata—the traditional wounds of Christ— probably is identifying intensely with the image of the crucified savior.

For Fodor, at-oneness, is a process by which a person projects his own characteristics onto a statue, picture, or some other inanimate object.

He believed that in genuine cases of weeping paintings of the Virgin Mary, for example, the tears actually were those of someone in the household. Somehow, sorrow or anguish which was not normally expressed was transposed onto the painting.

Is this what happened in the case of Canon Lewis' photograph of his grandmother? And if so, who really was weeping?

99. The Dead Pose for Their Portraits

Have you ever heard of "ghosts" sitting for their portraits?

In London, I visited Mrs. Coral Polge, a psychic artist specializing in sketches of the departed who, she says, obligingly model for her.

Mrs. Polge knew nothing about me. My appointment with her was made by a friend in the name of "Mr. Allen."

We had barely shaken hands at the front door of the medium's modest home in the London suburb of Twickenham, when she suddenly said: "I strongly feel the presence of your grandparents."

With that, she whisked me into the house, plopped me into a chair, grabbed a pencil and sketch pad, and began drawing furiously.

As she sketched, the medium described my maternal grandfather to me.

"He seems to have had sore feet," she muttered. "Must have walked a lot."

I grinned. My grandfather was a postman.

"He was a little downtrodden by his wife," she went on. "He couldn't manage money but he was very kindhearted. Liked his wee nip now and then."

She looked at me and smiled wryly.

"More than a wee nip sometimes, and more than now and then."

None of this was startling but it was accurate, so far as I knew. Though I had never seen my grandparents, my mother had told me a lot about them.

The sketch, that took no more than five minutes, seemed to bear so remarkable a likeness to a photograph of my grandfather that I almost gasped.

There was the drooping mustache, the fine-shaped nose, the high but not receded hairline. So far as I was concerned, the man in the sketch was an older version of the man in the picture that used to hang in my parent's home.

Coral Polge tore off the sheet and immediately started another sketch.

"This is your grandmother," she said. "She was a very strong-willed person. She had a shrewd business sense. Really, she did remarkably well in a financial way, though she had little enough to start with."

This description, too, seemed to fit.

Then, as the medium finished the drawing, she held it up, with a flourish, for me to see.

It was a striking likeness of my grandmother as she had stared out of her photograph at me when I was a child. Older, of course, but the firm, almost tyrannical set of the jaw was there, and the right, no-nonsense mouth.

Then the medium said: "Just a moment. She asks for one little change."

Erasing the mouth in the sketch, the medium redrew it—softer, with a hint of a smile.

The transformation was dramatic. Now the face was still formidable—obviously not a person to tangle with—but, at the same time, almost cherubic.

Said the medium: "Your grandmother wants you to know that she wasn't as bad as she sometimes may have seemed."

I confess to chuckling while trying to keep a straight face so as not to provide the medium with any sensory clues that could assist her with the sketches.

After leaving the medium's house, I wondered if the likeness to my grandparents was real or only fancied.

Would others also see it?

As soon as I arrived home, I got a part answer at least to that.

Without giving my wife an inkling of what I was up to, I took the medium's two sketches out of my suitcase and held them up.

"Your grandparents," my wife said with surprise. "Who on earth drew them?"

After a determined search we dug up the old photograph of my grandparents and compared it with the sketches. My wife and I agreed that there was a distinct—we felt, astonishing—similarity.

But how?

Did the medium base the sketches on some obscure family resemblance between my grandparents and me?

Did she pick the images from my mind by telepathy?

Or, is it even barely conceivable, that she was indeed sketching faces which, though invisible to everybody else, were visible to her.

Anyway, I hope my grandmother liked her picture

100. The Possession of Maria Talarico

In January, 1939, in the small Italian town of Siano, a 17-year-old girl apparently was possessed by the spirit of a dead man.

This extraordinary state of affairs came about one day when Maria Talarico, with her mother, was passing a spot where three years before a 19-year-old boy named Pepe Veraldi had been found dead. Suddenly, Maria complained of feeling faint. Her mother assisted her to the house and called the doctor. By the time he arrived Maria was in what appeared to be a coma.

Suddenly she roused and, in a harsh masculine voice snarled: "Get my dinner, I am Pepe."

The change in Maria was alarming. From being a well-brought up girl, she took up drinking and smoking. She swore like a man. She insisted that she was not Maria but Pepe—the youth who had died three years before.

Pepe had been found lying dead under a bridge on the outskirts of town, his clothes in disarray. It appeared that he had suffered a mental lapse, ripped his clothes, then leapt from the bridge to his death. The official verdict of suicide did not, however, entirely remove a suspicion of foul play.

Now the personality controlling Maria Talarico, and claiming to be Pepe, insisted vehemently that he had been killed in a brawl by four drinking companions.

Dr. Giovanni Scambia, a wise, experienced physician, did not know what to make of the case. Hysteria is not uncommon, of course, among teen-aged girls. But there were puzzling features in this case. Eerie features.

For one thing, the Pepe personality showed an uncanny familiarity with the dead youth's personal life. And for another, when the Pepe personality wrote a note to the dead boy's mother, Dr. Scambia compared the handwriting with a sample of Pepe's. The two matched, yet the girl Maria had never seen Pepe or his handwriting.

Moreover, when the dead youth's mother and other members of the family came to visit the possessed girl, they testified, in wonderment, that it was as though they were talking with Pepe.

Four medical consultants, called in besides Dr. Scambia, agreed in their diagnosis: Unknown.

On January 5, the Pepe personality suddenly demanded to be taken to the scene of his death.

Accompanied by Dr. Scambia and a small crowd, the girl Maria, still in the thrall of her macabre delusion, ran to the very spot under the bridge where Pepe's body had been found, tore off her clothes, and hurled herself on the ground. All this happened before any one could even move to restrain her. Then she lay still, deathlike.

A few minutes later Maria opened her brown eyes wide, looked around, and, in a small girlish voice, murmured: "What happened to me?"

Her question to this day, remains part of the unexplained . . .

About the Author

Allen Spraggett is a noted media personality in Canada. His column, "The Unexplained," is syndicated weekly in some sixty newspapers in Canada and the United States. He was host, during the 1974-75 television season, of two weekly programs on Canada's Global Television Network, including one called "ESP—Extra Special People." In 1967, Allen Spraggett arranged and hosted the now famous television séance between Bishop Pike and his son James, through the noted medium Arthur Ford.

Mr. Spraggett is the founder-president of the Toronto Society for Psychical Research, and has taught parapsychology at Toronto's Ryerson Polytechnical Institute. He lectures widely on the unexplained on college campuses and to packed audiences in the U.S. and in Canada.

Among Allen Spraggett's books for NAL are *Arthur Ford: The Man Who Talked with the Dead, The Case for Immortality,* and *The World of the Unexplained.*